For Early Learners

Clever Creations

Easy-to-Make Hands-On Learning Activities

Dottie Zimmermann

Thinking Publications • Eau Claire, Wisconsin

© 2001 by Thinking Publications

09   08   07   06   05   04   03   02   01   9   8   7   6   5   4   3   2   1

Library of Congress Cataloging-in-Publication Data
    Zimmermann, Dottie, date.
      Clever creations : easy-to-make hands-on learning activities / Dottie Zimmermann.
         p. cm.
    Includes bibliographical references.
    ISBN 1-888222-65-4 (pbk.)
      1. Early childhood education—Activity programs. I. Title.
    LB1139.35.A37 Z56 2001
    372.13—dc21   2001020270

Printed in the United States of America

Cover design by Kris Gausman

THINKING PUBLICATIONS®
A Division of McKinley Companies, Inc.

424 Galloway Street • Eau Claire, WI 54703
(715) 832-2488 • FAX (715) 832-9082
Email: custserv@ThinkingPublications.com

COMMUNICATION SOLUTIONS THAT CHANGE LIVES®

CONTENTS

Section 2: Storytelling Activities

Appendices

References

Preface

Although I was an extremely eager and excited first-year teacher, I was unprepared for the lack of developmentally appropriate materials in my classroom. That year I met Cindy Gebhart, who introduced me to the wonderful world of hands-on teacher-made materials for young children. I found I had a passion for envisioning, creating, and implementing these materials. Through a process of trial and error and implicit feedback from children (i.e., many materials spent a lifetime on the shelf because children never played with them), I was able to construct materials that were appropriate for the developmental levels of the young children in my class while supporting their play. I began to display and demonstrate my homemade materials at state and local education conferences. The enthusiastic responses from educators and parents encouraged me to put a collection of materials into a resource book. The result is *Clever Creations: Easy-to-Make Hands-On Learning Activities.*

I am very grateful to Linda Schreiber, editor at Thinking Publications, for her guidance, cheerful comments, and creative suggestions; however, I am most grateful for her undying support and contagious belief in this book.

I would like to give a special thanks to Liz Darby, Bobbie Dingess, Brandee Farrell, Cindy Gebhart, Kathy Kelchner, Margot Kelman, Kelly Lessman, Kay McGee, Robin Moran, Karen Miller, Jamilla Perry, Kathy Westmoreland, and Vicky Zimmermann for the time they spent reviewing this document and their gentle suggestions for improvement.

Many thanks should be given to the very special people at Chapel Hills Presbyterian Church and Preschool—I learned so much there. They are wonderful teachers, in and out of the classroom. I appreciate the ideas for *The Little Old Lady Who Swallowed a Fly, Three Billy Goats Gruff,* and *Hang It Up.*

And finally, I am so very grateful to my family—Mom, Pope, David, Vicky, and Michael—for their encouragement, love, and understanding. I am a very lucky person.

About the Author

Dottie Zimmermann has over 20 years of experience in education. She received her bachelor's of science degrees in elementary education and special education from the University of Texas in Austin and later received her certification in early-childhood education. She has taught preschool and kindergarten and was director of a preschool and a child development center. Dottie is currently the visiting teacher with the preschool program for children with disabilities at the Richardson Independent School District in Texas. Dottie has been presenting at professional workshops for over 15 years and has written over 50 Interactive Songbooks. She is married to David and is the very proud mother of 18-year-old Vicky (Little Girl) and 12-year-old Michael (Handsomest Dude). Dottie is an avid reader and a quasi quilter; she enjoys cross-stitching and outings with "The Fat Five."

Introduction

Overview

"Children are active learners who thrive on first-hand experiences" (Ard and Pitts, 1995, p. 2). Through play, children learn about their world, themselves, and others. They learn best by touching, holding, observing, listening, and experimenting with the materials in their environment. Child-initiated, child-directed, teacher-supported play is an essential component of developmentally appropriate practice (Houser and Osborne, n.d.).

Clever Creations: Easy-to-Make Hands-On Activities guides you in preparing a variety of learning experiences that fit the characteristics described by the National Association for the Education of Young Children (NAEYC, 1997) as necessary for a developmentally appropriate program. Children need a balance of many types of activities and experiences. They need opportunities to construct their own understanding of the world through exploration, and they also benefit from guidance in their learning from more competent peers and adults. Children need predictable structure and orderly routine in their learning environment, yet the teacher must remain flexible in responding to their emerging and changing ideas, needs, and interests. Children need opportunities to make meaningful choices regarding activities, yet they must understand that available choices reside within clear boundaries. Young children need to be challenged to work on new tasks but also need plenty of opportunity to practice familiar skills and to develop persistence in working on a task. While children need opportunities to engage in self-initiated spontaneous play, they also need educator-planned and educator-structured activities, projects, and experiences.

Clever Creations was written as a guide for early-childhood educators, preschool teachers, speech-language pathologists, and parents for creating inexpensive, developmentally appropriate activities to use with young children. Activities described in this manual provide opportunities for children who are at a preschool level (approximately ages 2–6) to play, work, and learn in a developmentally appropriate manner. Activities are listed by age in the *Cross-Reference Chart by Age* on pages 10–11.

An Ideal Early-Childhood Program

Clever Creations can help you provide the 10 characteristics of a great early-childhood program (NAEYC, 1996b):

1. **Children play and work with items or other children.** They do not wander without a purpose or sit inactive for long periods of time. *Clever Creations* provides ideas for you to add materials and activities to your classroom that will keep children engaged in purpose-

ful, meaningful play. The hands-on nature of these activities ensures that children are learning in an appropriate context, individually or with peers.

2. **Children are given access to many activities and materials all day; they do not all do the same things at the same time.** Managing the many demands for the educator's attention can be a challenge in a program for young children. Activities from *Clever Creations* provide children with many choices that they can manage independently after an introduction by an adult.

3. **Educators work with individuals, small groups, and the whole group at times throughout the day rather than only in whole-group activities.** Activities and materials from *Clever Creations* are designed for use with individuals, small groups, or large groups. Children and educators have increased flexibility in the classroom to interact as needed when they use these materials and activities. The educator may introduce an activity to a group so that children are familiar with how to use it, but the hands-on learning activities in *Clever Creations* are also intended for individual and small-group exploration by children. The storytelling activities can be educator directed but following story presentation, retelling can be child directed.

4. **Educators decorate the classroom with artwork done by children.** Activities from *Clever Creations* will be a springboard for children's own creations. Writing and drawing materials should always be available in the classroom, so children can write or draw about what they have made and learned. For example, when children tell stories using one of the flannel boards described (see pages 132–139), they can write and draw about their stories as well. When children explore the texture of objects using *This Feels Like…* (see pages 112–113), they can draw pictures of what they think is inside the can. Remember that decorations in the classroom should emphasize children's creations rather than commercial or educator-made items and should be located at a height where children can enjoy them (Cryer and Phillipsen, 1997).

5. **Knowledge of numbers and alphabet letters is incorporated into children's everyday experiences. Exploring plants and animals, cooking, taking attendance, and serving snacks are all meaningful activities to children.** Every activity in *Clever Creations* allows children to explore and learn concepts in playful, meaningful contexts. Drill and practice is not recommended with these materials. For example, *Happy Birthday* (see pages 60–61) allows children to explore the concept of one-to-one correspondence by encouraging them to count candles to match the number on a birthday card. Children who are learning to read numbers or count can use these materials with adult guidance and can relate the activity of counting birthday candles to real life.

6. **Children have time to work on specific activities and to play and explore. Worksheets are seldom used, if ever.** The activities in *Clever Creations* will keep children engaged for extended periods of time with high-interest materials and themes. Children may spend a short period of time with one activity, but there will be many other activities for them to choose from during their activity period. The educator may choose to extend an activity by guiding children in writing or drawing about what they have learned.

7. **Children are allowed to play outside daily, weather permitting. Instructional time is not substituted for outside play.** *Outside/Inside* (see pages 84–85) encourages children to explore new activities outside and develop language skills to discuss their experiences. Other activities, like *Planting Flowers* (see pages 92–93), may be logical companions to units that involve children in outside adventures.

8. **Educators read books to children at group story time and throughout the day.** *Clever Creations* includes a section of Storytelling Activities. This section uses storytelling props and displays to expand on the experiences shared with children and books. It includes props such as flannel boards, story card pocket aprons, and story cards. Many of the hands-on learning activities—like *Mmmm! Gingerbread* (see pages 80–81) or *Ladybug, Ladybug, Fly Away Home* (see pages 68–69)—could also be tied to books and story reading. These activities encourage children to do their own storytelling and sharing in addition to enjoying story presentations.

9. **Educators adapt the curriculum for children who are advanced and for children who need extra help. Children have different learning styles due to different backgrounds.** The activities in *Clever Creations* are open-ended, so preschool children in a broad developmental range can use them in meaningful ways. In addition to children with typical variations in learning, children with special needs are successful with the activities. Rather than needing highly specialized materials to include children with special needs in a program, educators report that children need support from peers and specialists, a willingness to adapt to new environments, and positive relationships with families (NAEYC, 1996a). A source for further information on successful inclusion of children with disabilities may be found online from the National Information Center for Children and Youth with Disabilities *(http://nichcy.org/).*

10. **Children are eager to go to school. Children and parents have safe and happy feelings about school.** Using *Clever Creations* will encourage children to have fun, develop their independence, and interact positively with peers. Parents will appreciate the colorful, inventive materials and activities they see throughout the classroom.

The classroom will provide the security of organized materials and structured activity, while allowing for regular changes in the type and variety of experiences available.

How *Clever Creations* Is Organized

Sections

Section 1: Learning Activities contains the information you will need to construct learning activities for use with young children. These developmentally appropriate, educator-made learning activities supplement and enrich the curriculum. For example, if studying a transportation theme, these activities could be used to supplement the unit of study: *The Key to It All* (see pages 66–67) and *Park It Here* (see pages 88–89). The *Cross-Reference Chart by Theme* on pages 16–19 will help you locate activities based on themes.

Likewise, the activities can be used to reinforce specific skills. For example, if a child needs to develop fine-motor coordination, encourage him or her to explore *Gone Fishin'* (see pages 54–55), *Mmmm! Gingerbread* (see pages 80–81), or *Super Scooper* (see pages 110–111). The use of *Pick a Pocket* (pages 90–91) or *A Very Simple Cookie Cutter Puzzle* (see pages 120–121) reinforces a child's ability to match items. Skills addressed in each activity are listed in the *Cross-Reference Chart by Skill* on pages 12–15 for easy reference.

Section 2: Storytelling Activities details information for construction of props for songs, fingerplays, and stories. Children are actively involved with the manipulation of props, as in *Three Billy Goats Gruff* (see pages 172–176), hand motions, as in *The Itsy Bitsy Spider* (see pages 142–145), and the anticipation of the verses in stories, as in *The Little Old Lady Who Swallowed a Fly* (see pages 150–153). Storytelling sessions will be enhanced by using these materials, and children will be encouraged to present their own stories when they use the materials independently.

Format of the Activities

Each activity in this book uses an organizational format that includes the following:

- *Instructional Settings*—lists a suggested group size (i.e., large group, small group, or independent play) for each activity. Large group activities are for a group of 6 to 10 children, small group activities are for a group of 2–5 children, and independent play refers to a child playing with the activity with or without adult support. These group sizes are only suggestions. Depending on the size of your class and the developmental level of the children in your class, you may wish to adjust the number of children for an activity.

- *Skills*—lists the educational component of the activity. Use the skills listed as a guide when selecting activities for children's specific needs or when addressing a child's individualized educational program (IEP) goals and objectives. For example, if a child does not recognize or identify numerals to five, *Box It Up* (see pages 30–31) could be used to determine if he or she can count to five with one-to-one correspondence. When the child is successful at counting, *Hang It Up* (see pages 58–59) could be used to reinforce counting with one-to-one correspondence and recognizing and identifying numerals to five. The skills included in *Clever Creations* are listed in the *Cross-Reference Chart by Skills* on pages 12–15 for your convenience.

- *Themes*—describes how the activity might fit into curriculum themes or units of study. A single learning activity may be applicable to a variety of themes. You can locate activities by theme by using the *Cross-Reference Chart by Theme* on pages 16–19.

- *Materials*—lists suggestions for the items needed to make the activity or prop. Items listed are easily obtained and are inexpensive or free! Most can be found around the school or classroom. Goodwill, Dollar Stores, garage sales, and rummage sales are a wonderful source for materials at a reasonable cost.

    Some of the items referenced can be substituted with other suitable items. If you do not have access to a laminator, use clear Contac paper. Instead of poster board, use old file folders. Appendix A includes a letter to send to families requesting that they send recyclable materials your way. When required, art patterns are also provided in Appendix B.

- *Preparation*—details the directions for assembling the learning activity or prop. Step-by-step instructions are provided to help you prepare each activity or prop. When making the activities or props, remember to gather all the materials and supplies, read all the directions before beginning, and save the patterns. A photograph to aid with the assembly is provided as the lead-in to all activities.

- *Activity*—includes suggested directions for using the learning activity or prop. All the learning materials emphasize hands-on, active learning and include a communication component that helps children develop their understanding and use of concepts, vocabulary, and relationships. Introduce the activity to the children in a small or large group to ensure each child understands how to use the materials. By observing children actively engaged with the material, you may be able to assess the strengths and learning needs of each child and give immediate feedback. After you feel the children are familiar with the activity, place it on a shelf for independent play. The activity can usually be judged a success if a child is actively engaged with the task and stays involved for an amount of time appropriate for his or her developmental age.

- *A Little Something Else*—lists possible ways to extend the idea presented in order to provide continued growth and expansion of interests. On occasion, the activity can be adapted to pull in concepts from a theme being studied in the classroom. When this is workable, suggestions are given.

- *Notes*—provides a place to write notes regarding the activity. Notes might include adaptations to the activity, a related material (e.g., a storybook) you have added, materials you have substituted, and so on. (Note that because of space constraints, a few activities do not include a Notes area.)

Age guidelines for each activity are included in the *Cross-Reference Chart by Age* on pages 10–11. The guidelines are based on the experience and knowledge of the author; you may make adaptations to the ideas to include a broader range of developmental levels and abilities. Safety for young children is of utmost importance. Use your judgment in determining the developmental age of children and the safety of the materials and activities listed in this book. If children in your care tend to put things in their mouths, avoid activities that have small pieces. Although every effort has been made to ensure the safety of the items presented, it is ultimately your responsibility to ensure the safety of children who use these materials.

How to Arrange the Activities

Proper storage of learning materials in the classroom is an important element in encouraging independence in children and creating an effective learning environment. On occasion, a storage container is suggested in the learning activities. If not suggested, however, materials should be stored in clear (such as clear plastic shoeboxes) or open containers and placed on low, open shelving or other locations easily accessible to children. Clear or open containers work best for storage because children can easily see the materials in the container. When cardboard boxes are used for storage, it is important to label the box with a picture of the item, so children can "read" what is inside (Ard and Pitts, 1995).

It is also important to label the container and the shelf where the container goes with identical labels so children can select and then return the materials successfully. Use labeling that is meaningful to the children, such as a small piece of the activity itself, a photograph, drawings, or photocopies. Have a special container (a box or a bowl) available for the children to put stray pieces (such as puzzle pieces, flannel board pieces, and other game pieces) for weekly sorting. It is easier for children to keep small pieces organized and within reach when you provide individual workspaces (e.g., a small carpet, cafeteria tray, or a table and chair) for them. Remember to check the learning activities frequently to be sure that they are complete and unbroken. The learning activity will not be stimulating for children if it is broken or has missing pieces. Remove broken or incomplete activities until pieces can be replaced or materials can be repaired.

The learning activities presented in *Clever Creations* are open-ended, thus allowing materials to be used in a variety of ways. Use the information in this book as a springboard for your own innovative ideas, and see what creativity can produce!

Cross-Reference Chart by Age	Page	Developmental Age				
		2	3	4	5	6
Section 1: Learning Activities						
Baby Bootie Match	22	X	X			
Beauty Shop on the Go	24		X	X	X	X
Bits and Pieces	26		X	X	X	X
Boo-Boo Cover-Ups	28			X	X	X
Box It Up	30		X	X	X	X
Cha-Cha Chains	32		X	X	X	X
Chocolate Chippers	34			X	X	X
Clip It	36		X	X	X	
Curler Cutouts	38	X	X	X	X	
Dish It Up	40	X	X	X	X	
Donut Match	42		X	X	X	X
Do You Hear What I Hear?	44		X	X	X	X
Dreamers	46	X	X	X	X	X
Eraser Match	48		X	X	X	X
Fabric Match	50	X	X	X	X	X
Gadget Match	52		X	X	X	X
Gone Fishing	54	X	X	X	X	X
Hang It Here	56		X	X	X	X
Hang It Up	58		X	X	X	
Happy Birthday	60			X	X	X
Hide and Seek	62	X	X	X		
Jingle Pocket	64		X	X	X	X
The Key to It All	66		X	X	X	X
Ladybug, Ladybug, Fly Away Home	68		X	X	X	X
Mac and Cheese Please	70		X	X	X	X
McFries	72		X	X	X	X
Making Faces	74	X	X	X	X	X
McNugget Munch	76			X	X	X
Mirror Magic	78		X	X	X	X
Mmmm! Gingerbread	80			X	X	X
Name/Picture Match	82		X	X	X	X
Outside/Inside	84	X	X	X	X	X
Pack a Pencil Bag	86		X	X	X	X
Park It Here	88			X	X	X

Cross-Reference Chart by Age

Continued

	Page	Developmental Age				
		2	3	4	5	6
Section 1: Learning Activities						
Pick a Pocket	90		X	X	X	X
Planting Flowers	92	X	X	X	X	X
Popcorn Fun	94			X	X	X
Puppet Pals	96	X	X	X	X	
Scrubber Number	98			X	X	X
Sinker and Floater	100		X	X	X	X
Smelly Jars	102		X	X	X	X
Soap It Up	104		X	X	X	X
Sock It to Me	106	X	X	X	X	
Star Gazing	108	X	X	X	X	X
Super Scooper	110		X	X	X	X
This Feels Like…	112		X	X	X	X
Toothbrush Tango	114	X	X	X	X	X
Touch and Tell	116	X	X	X	X	X
Touch Book	118	X	X	X	X	X
A Very Simple Cookie Cutter Puzzle	120	X	X	X		
What's That Picture?	122	X	X	X	X	X
Section 2: Storytelling Activities						
Chicka Boom	126		X	X	X	X
Five Green and Speckled Frogs	128	X	X	X	X	X
Flannel Board: Fabric Bolt	132	X	X	X	X	X
Flannel Board: Pizza Box	134	X	X	X	X	X
Flannel Board: School-Supply Box	136	X	X	X	X	X
Flannel Board: Wallpaper Book	138	X	X	X	X	X
Fold and Play Prop	140		X	X	X	X
The Itsy Bitsy Spider	142					
Little Dude and His Funny Face	146	X	X	X	X	X
The Little Old Lady Who Swallowed a Fly	150	X	X	X	X	X
Lunch at the Deli	154			X	X	X
Peanut Butter and Jelly	158	X	X	X	X	X
Seven in the Bed	160	X	X	X	X	X
A Sticky Situation	164	X	X	X	X	X
Story Card Pocket Apron	166	X	X	X	X	X
Story Cards	168	X	X	X	X	X
Story Card Stage	170	X	X	X	X	X
Three Billy Goats Gruff	172	X	X	X	X	X

Cross-Reference Chart by Skill

Section 1: Learning Activities	Page	Developing fine-motor coordination	Developing self-awareness	Discriminating size, shape, texture	Matching	Sorting	Recognizing/Identifying: • colors	• full/empty	• same/different	• shapes	• sizes	• slow/fast	• textures	Counting with 1-to-1 corr:	Ordering by number	Recognizing/Identifying: • more/less	• numerals to 5	• numerals to 10
							Quality							*Quantity*				
Baby Bootie Match	22				X	X	X		X	X								
Beauty Shop on the Go	24	X			X	X	X		X									
Bits and Pieces	26			X														
Boo-Boo Cover-Ups	28	X					X							X	X			X
Box It Up	30	X									X			X	X		X	
Cha-Cha Chains	32	X		X								X						
Chocolate Chippers	34													X	X			X
Clip It	36	X			X		X	X										
Curler Cutouts	38	X		X	X							X						
Dish It Up	40	X			X		X											
Donut Match	42				X		X		X						X			
Do You Hear What I Hear?	44				X		X											
Dreamers	46	X									X							
Eraser Match	48	X		X	X				X									
Fabric Match	50			X	X				X	X					X			
Gadget Match	52	X		X	X													
Gone Fishin'	54	X					X											
Hang It Here	56	X												X	X			X
Hang It Up	58													X	X		X	
Happy Birthday	60	X												X	X			X
Hide and Seek	62			X	X													
Jingle Pocket	64			X										X				X
The Key to It All	66	X		X	X													
Ladybug, Ladybug, Fly Away Home	68													X	X	X		X
Mac and Cheese Please	70	X												X	X	X		X
McFries	72	X												X	X			X
Making Faces	74	X	X															
McNugget Munch	76													X	X			X
Mirror Magic	78		X				X		X	X								
Mmmm! Gingerbread	80	X					X							X	X	X		X
Name/Picture Match	82	X	X	X	X													
Outside/Inside	84				X													
Pack a Pencil Bag	86	X			X	X	X											
Park It Here	88	X												X	X			X

Cross-Reference Chart by Skill

Continued

Preliteracy

	Page	Describing feelings	Describing using senses	Ordering by size	Determining cause and effect	Listening	Naming: • objects and their functions	• objects by category	Predicting	Recognizing part-whole	Developing sound-symbol corr:	Recognizing/identifying: • Alphabet letters	• Words	Rhyming	Retelling a story/song/chant
Section 1: Learning Activities															
Baby Bootie Match	22														
Beauty Shop on the Go	24					X									
Bits and Pieces	26								X	X	X				
Boo-Boo Cover-Ups	28														
Box It Up	30														
Cha-Cha Chains	32		X												
Chocolate Chippers	34		X												
Clip It	36						X								
Curler Cutouts	38						X	X							
Dish It Up	40														
Donut Match	42		X						X						
Do You Hear What I Hear?	44		X									X			
Dreamers	46				X										
Eraser Match	48						X								
Fabric Match	50		X				X								
Gadget Match	52		X												
Gone Fishin'	54														
Hang It Here	56		X												
Hang It Up	58														
Happy Birthday	60	X													
Hide and Seek	62		X												
Jingle Pocket	64		X									X			
The Key to It All	66		X												
Ladybug, Ladybug, Fly Away Home	68	X							X						
Mac and Cheese Please	70														
McFries	72								X						
Making Faces	74	X													
McNugget Munch	76		X						X						
Mirror Magic	78		X		X							X			
Mmmm! Gingerbread	80							X							
Name/Picture Match	82														
Outside/Inside	84	X							X	X			X		
Pack a Pencil Bag	86							X							
Park It Here	88								X						

Continued on next page

Cross-Reference Chart by Skill
Continued

	Page	Developing fine-motor coordination	Developing self-awareness	Discriminating size, shape, texture	Matching	Sorting	Recognizing/Identifying: • colors	• full/empty	• same/different	• shapes	• sizes	• slow/fast	• textures	Counting with 1-to-1 corr:	Ordering by number	Recognizing/Identifying: • more/less	• numerals to 5	• numerals to 10
							Quality							Quantity				
Pick a Pocket	90	X		X	X		X			X								
Planting Flowers	92	X			X		X											
Popcorn Fun	94				X									X				
Puppet Pals	96		X															
Scrubber Number	98	X												X	X	X		X
Sinker and Floater	100	X				X												
Smelly Jars	102				X				X									
Soap It Up	104				X		X											
Sock It to Me	106			X	X	X								X	X			
Star Gazing	108																	
Super Scooper	110	X					X	X						X				
This Feels Like…	112			X														
Toothbrush Tango	114				X		X											
Touch and Tell	116	X		X	X				X				X					
Touch Book	118												X					
A Very Simple Cookie Cutter Puzzle	120			X	X						X	X						
What's That Picture?	122																	
Section 2: Storytelling Activities																		
Chicka Boom	126																	
Five Green and Speckled Frogs	128	X												X				
Flannel Board: Fabric Bolt	132	X			X										X			
Flannel Board: Pizza Box	134	X			X										X			
Flannel Board: School-Supply Box	136	X			X										X			
Flannel Board: Wallpaper Book	138	X			X										X			
Fold and Play Prop	140																	
The Itsy Bitsy Spider	142	X																
Little Dude and His Funny Face	146	X	X				X											
The Little Old Lady Who Swallowed a Fly	150																	
Lunch at the Deli	154	X																
Peanut Butter and Jelly	158	X																
Seven in the Bed	160	X													X			
A Sticky Situation	164												X					
Story Card Pocket Apron	166	X																
Story Cards	168																	
Story Card Stage	170	X																
Three Billy Goats Gruff	172	X									X							

Cross-Reference Chart by Skill

Continued

	Page	Describing feelings	Describing using senses	Ordering by size	Determining cause and effect	Listening	Naming: • objects and their functions	• objects by category	Predicting	Recognizing part-whole	Developing sound-symbol corr:	Preliteracy — Recognizing/identifying: • Alphabet letters	• Words	Rhyming	Retelling a story/song/chant
Section 1: Learning Activities															
Pick a Pocket	90						X								
Planting Flowers	92		X				X	X							
Popcorn Fun	94						X					X			
Puppet Pals	96	X					X								X
Scrubber Number	98		X			X									
Sinker and Floater	100				X				X						
Smelly Jars	102	X	X						X						
Soap It Up	104		X												
Sock It to Me	106		X												
Star Gazing	108				X				X						
Super Scooper	110														
This Feels Like…	112		X				X		X						
Toothbrush Tango	114						X	X							
Touch and Tell	116		X												
Touch Book	118		X										X		
A Very Simple Cookie Cutter Puzzle	120			X											
What's That Picture?	122						X			X	X				
Section 2: Storytelling Activities															
Chicka Boom	126					X					X	X			X
Five Green and Speckled Frogs	128					X								X	X
Flannel Board: Fabric Bolt	132					X									X
Flannel Board: Pizza Box	134					X									X
Flannel Board: School-Supply Box	136					X									X
Flannel Board: Wallpaper Book	138					X									X
Fold and Play Prop	140					X									X
The Itsy Bitsy Spider	142					X									X
Little Dude and His Funny Face	146	X	X			X									X
The Little Old Lady Who Swallowed a Fly	150				X	X			X					X	X
Lunch at the Deli	154	X				X	X	X					X		
Peanut Butter and Jelly	158	X				X									X
Seven in the Bed	160	X				X								X	X
A Sticky Situation	164		X		X										X
Story Card Pocket Apron	166					X									X
Story Cards	168					X									X
Story Card Stage	170					X									X
Three Billy Goats Gruff	172	X				X			X						X

Cross-Reference Chart by Theme

Section 1: Learning Activities	Body parts	Boxes and bows	Celebrations	Clothing	Colors	Community helpers	Cookies	Fairy tales	Families	Farm animals	Feelings	Flowers	Food	Friends	Gardening	Health	Holidays	I'm me	Insects	Letters
Baby Bootie Match	X			X	X															
Beauty Shop on the Go				X	X	X														
Bits and Pieces																				
Boo-Boo Cover-Ups				X	X											X				
Box It Up		X	X														X			
Cha-Cha Chains				X	X															
Chocolate Chippers					X	X							X							
Clip It				X	X															
Curler Cutouts					X															
Dish It Up				X												X				
Donut Match				X	X								X							
Do You Hear What I Hear?																				
Dreamers																X				
Eraser Match																				
Fabric Match				X		X														
Gadget Match																				
Gone Fishin'				X																X
Hang It Here				X	X	X														
Hang It Up				X																
Happy Birthday		X	X								X							X		
Hide and Seek																				
Jingle Pocket																	X			
The Key to It All						X														
Ladybug, Ladybug, Fly Away Home												X			X				X	
Mac and Cheese Please		X								X			X							
McFries													X			X				
Making Faces	X									X	X							X		
McNugget Munch													X							
Mirror Magic	X				X													X		
Mmmm! Gingerbread				X			X						X				X			
Name/Picture Match														X				X		
Outside/Inside																				
Pack a Pencil Bag				X																
Park It Here																				

Cross-Reference Chart by Theme

Continued

Section 1: Learning Activities	Light and dark	Multiple themes	My neighborhood	Night and day	Numbers	Nursery rhymes	Outside/Inside	Ponds	Reptiles	School	Seasons	Senses	Shapes	Space	Transportation	Water fun	Weather
Baby Bootie Match																	
Beauty Shop on the Go			X														
Bits and Pieces		X															
Boo-Boo Cover-Ups					X								X				
Box It Up					X								X				
Cha-Cha Chains													X				
Chocolate Chippers			X		X												
Clip It					X												
Curler Cutouts			X														
Dish It Up					X												
Donut Match			X		X												
Do You Hear What I Hear?							X					X					
Dreamers											X					X	
Eraser Match		X			X					X			X				
Fabric Match												X	X				
Gadget Match		X											X				
Gone Fishin'					X			X					X			X	
Hang It Here					X												
Hang It Up					X												
Happy Birthday					X												
Hide and Seek	X												X				
Jingle Pocket												X					
The Key to It All															X		
Ladybug, Ladybug, Fly Away Home					X		X			X							
Mac and Cheese Please					X												
McFries			X		X												
Making Faces												X					
McNugget Munch			X		X												
Mirror Magic													X				
Mmmm! Gingerbread					X												
Name/Picture Match		X								X							
Outside/Inside							X				X						X
Pack a Pencil Bag					X					X							
Park It Here			X		X										X		

Continued on next page

Cross-Reference Chart by Theme

Continued

	Body parts	Boxes and bows	Celebrations	Clothing	Colors	Community helpers	Cookies	Fairy tales	Families	Farm animals	Feelings	Flowers	Food	Friends	Gardening	Health	Holidays	I'm me	Insects	Letters
Section 1: Learning Activities																				
Pick a Pocket					X															
Planting Flowers					X							X			X					
Popcorn Fun													X							X
Puppet Pals						X		X	X			X						X		
Scrubber Number																				
Sinker and Floater																				
Smelly Jars											X	X								
Soap It Up					X											X		X		X
Sock It to Me	X			X	X															
Star Gazing																				
Super Scooper					X								X							
This Feels Like…																				
Toothbrush Tango	X				X	X										X				
Touch and Tell				X																
Touch Book				X																
A Very Simple Cookie Cutter Puzzle							X						X				X			
What's That Picture?																				
Section 2: Storytelling Activities																				
Chicka Boom								X												X
Five Green and Speckled Frogs																				
Flannel Board: Fabric Bolt																				
Flannel Board: Pizza Box																				
Flannel Board: School-Supply Box																				
Flannel Board: Wallpaper Book																				
Fold and Play Prop																				
The Itsy Bitsy Spider																			X	
Little Dude and His Funny Face	X				X									X						
The Little Old Lady Who Swallowed a Fly									X	X									X	
Lunch at the Deli						X							X						X	
Peanut Butter and Jelly													X							
Seven in the Bed											X			X						
A Sticky Situation																				
Story Card Pocket Apron																				
Story Cards																				
Story Card Stage																				
Three Billy Goats Gruff								X												

Cross-Reference Chart by Theme

Continued

	Light and dark	Multiple themes	My neighborhood	Night and day	Numbers	Nursery rhymes	Outside/Inside	Ponds	Reptiles	School	Seasons	Senses	Shapes	Space	Transportation	Water fun	Weather
Section 1: Learning Activities																	
Pick a Pocket		X											X				
Planting Flowers							X				X	X					
Popcorn Fun			X	X													
Puppet Pals																	
Scrubber Number				X								X					
Sinker and Floater								X			X					X	
Smelly Jars												X					
Soap It Up				X													
Sock It to Me																	
Star Gazing	X			X			X							X			
Super Scooper				X													
This Feels Like…		X										X					
Toothbrush Tango																	
Touch and Tell								X				X					
Touch Book												X					
A Very Simple Cookie Cutter Puzzle													X				
What's That Picture?		X															
Section 2: Storytelling Activities																	
Chicka Boom																	
Five Green and Speckled Frogs						X	X	X									
Flannel Board: Fabric Bolt		X															
Flannel Board: Pizza Box		X															
Flannel Board: School-Supply Box		X															
Flannel Board: Wallpaper Book		X															
Fold and Play Prop		X	X														
The Itsy Bitsy Spider							X					X					X
Little Dude and His Funny Face				X													
The Little Old Lady Who Swallowed a Fly																	
Lunch at the Deli																	
Peanut Butter and Jelly																	
Seven in the Bed			X	X													
A Sticky Situation		X															
Story Card Pocket Apron		X															
Story Cards		X															
Story Card Stage		X															
Three Billy Goats Gruff																	

Section 1

• • •

Learning Activities

• • •

BABY BOOTIE MATCH

Instructional Settings

Independent play

Small group (2–5 children)

Large group (6–10 children)

Skills

Recognizing/Identifying same/different

Recognizing/Identifying colors

Recognizing/Identifying shapes

Sorting

Matching

Themes

Body parts

Clothing

Colors

Materials

- Several pair of soft infant shoes in a variety of sizes, colors, and designs
- Shoebox

Preparation

None

Activity

Have children sort the shoes according to pairs. Encourage children to describe the shoes using descriptive words for the colors, designs, and shapes as they discuss how the shoes are different and how the shoes are the same. Show children how to place the booties back in the shoebox when finished.

A Little Something Else

Have children look at each other's shoes. Then have children take their shoes off and mix them up in a pile in the middle of the group. Have children sort the shoes and then try to name who each pair belongs to.

Notes

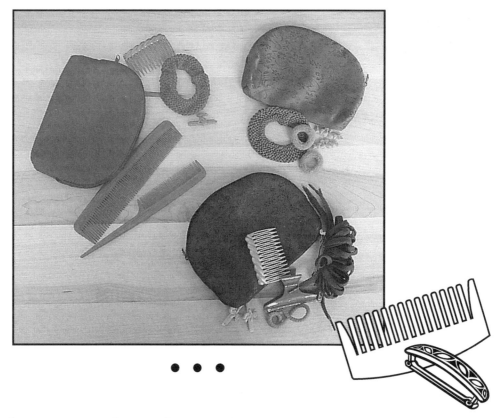

• • •

BEAUTY SHOP ON THE GO

Instructional Settings

Independent play

Small group (2–5 children)

Skills

Matching

Developing fine-motor coordination

Recognizing/Identifying colors

Naming objects and their functions

Sorting

Recognizing/Identifying same/different

Themes

Community helpers

Clothing

Colors

My neighborhood

Materials

- Red, green, and blue:
    - barrettes
    - ponytail holders
    - decorative hair combs
    - hair scrunchies
    - bows
    - ribbons
    - combs
    - brushes
    - curlers
    - makeup bags
- Container

Preparation

Place the hair accessories and the makeup bags in the container.

Activity

Have children remove the items from the container and sort the hair accessories into the make-up bags according to color. Have children name the items and the colors of the items and describe the uses for each. Encourage children to describe a person in their community who might use these items (e.g., a beautician) and where in their neighborhood they would find such a person. Show children how to put the materials in the container when finished.

A Little Something Else

Expand this activity to include additional colors, or have children choose a card with a numeral printed on it and put that many colored objects in a makeup bag (e.g., 5 red ponytail holders in the red bag or 3 green bows in the green bag). Create a beauty shop in your room, including dolls, capes, old electric razors, large chairs, empty plastic bottles, a cash register, old hair dryers and curling irons (with the cords cut off), and the items listed in the Materials list.

Notes

BITS AND PIECES

Instructional Settings

Independent play

Small group (2–5 children)

Skills

Matching

Predicting

Naming objects by category

Recognizing part/whole

Theme

Multiple themes

Materials

- Scissors
- 8½" × 11" heavy stock paper
- Glue
- Pictures of objects that are familiar to children and pictures of parts of those objects (e.g., door/doorknob, bus/wheel, chair/chair legs, bed/headboard, stove/burner, computer/keyboard, pencil/eraser, bathtub/faucet, tree/leaf, flower/petal, bike/pedal, and book/page)

Preparation

1. Cut the heavy stock paper in half.
2. Glue one picture on each half.
3. Laminate the pictures.

Activity

Have children match a card with a "whole" object to a card with the "part" of the object. Have children predict what the whole object might be if they have the part and what the part might be when they have the whole. Encourage children to name each whole object and its part. Then ask them to name one more part of the whole.

A Little Something Else

Make the activity more challenging by using photographs of objects and object parts that are less familiar to children (e.g., car/engine, bed/box spring, bike/gears, oven/oven rack, jeans/zipper, and dryer/lint basket). Or emphasize a particular theme by using pictures of objects related to the theme.

Notes

BOO-BOO COVER-UPS

Instructional Settings

Independent play

Small group (2–5 children)

Skills

Recognizing/Identifying numerals to 10

Recognizing/Identifying colors

Ordering by number

Counting with one-to-one correspondence

Developing fine-motor coordination

Naming objects by category

Determining cause and effect

Themes

Numbers

Health

Community helpers

Shapes

Colors

Materials

- *Bandage Pattern* (see Appendix B, page 181)
- Heavy stock paper
- Red and blue watercolor markers
- Black fine-point permanent marker
- Scissors
- Empty Band-Aid box (plastic boxes will last longer)

Preparation

1. Duplicate the *Bandage Pattern* onto heavy stock paper to create 22 bandages.
2. Color 11 strips blue and 11 strips red.
3. On the red bandage strips, write the numerals 0–10 (i.e., numeral 0 on one bandage, numeral 1 on another, and so on).
4. On the blue bandage strips, draw 1–10 dots (i.e., 0 dots on one bandage, 1 dot on another, and so on), leaving one bandage without dots.
5. Cut out the bandages.
6. Laminate the bandages.
7. Place the bandages in the Band-Aid box.

Activity

Have children match the red bandages with numerals to the corresponding blue bandages with dots. Show children how to put the bandages in numerical order. Encourage children to discuss who uses bandages and why bandages are used. Have children name the colors of the bandages. Show children how to store the bandages in the Band-Aid box when finished.

A Little Something Else

Make additional bandages containing shapes or colors for children to match.

Notes

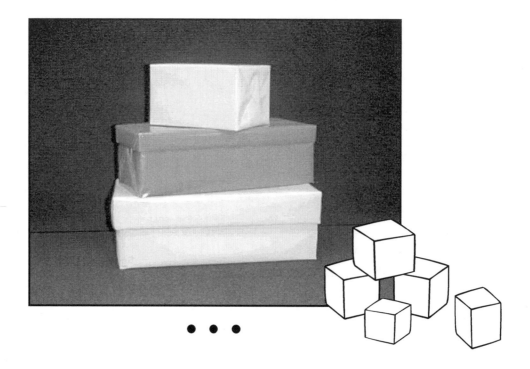

BOX IT UP

Instructional Settings

Independent play

Small group (2–5 children)

Skills

Ordering by number

Counting with one-to-one correspondence

Recognizing/Identifying numerals to 5

Recognizing/Identifying sizes

Developing fine-motor coordination

Ordering by size

Themes

Boxes and bows

Shapes

Numbers

Holidays

Celebrations

Materials

- 5 shoeboxes (including covers) of graduated sizes (e.g., infant shoebox, child's shoebox, youth shoebox, adult shoebox, and boot box; available free from most shoe stores)
- Wrapping paper or Contac paper
- Black fine-point permanent marker
- 15–20, 2" cube-shaped blocks

Preparation

1. Cover each shoebox and lid with wrapping paper or Contac paper.
2. Write the numerals 1–5 on the inside covers of the shoeboxes (i.e., numeral 1 on the smallest cover and numeral 5 on the largest cover).
3. Place the blocks in the smallest shoebox; then nest the shoeboxes together.

Activity

Tell children to open all the shoeboxes and dump the blocks out of the smallest shoebox. Have children look at the numeral on each cover, place that quantity of blocks in each shoebox, and put the covers back on each shoebox. Show children how to stack the shoeboxes according to size (first stacking from big to little and then reversing the order [if possible] by stacking from little to big). Have children talk about how the boxes fit inside one another using the terms *big, little, medium sized, bigger, biggest,* and so on. Show children how to store all the boxes inside one another when finished.

A Little Something Else

Make this activity more challenging by giving children an assortment of boxes and having them find the ones that nest inside each other. Cover the boxes in birthday or holiday wrapping paper to incorporate various themes.

Notes

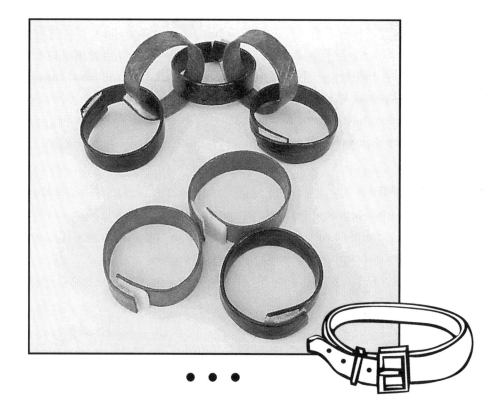

CHA-CHA CHAINS

Instructional Settings

Independent play

Small group (2–5 children)

Skills

Recognizing/Identifying textures

Describing using senses

Developing fine-motor coordination

Discriminating size, shape, texture

Themes

Shapes

Colors

Clothing

Materials

- Scissors
- Several different belts (available at thrift stores and garage sales)
- Velcro (available at fabric stores)
- Hot glue gun
- Container

Preparation

1. Cut the belts into 4" pieces.
2. Cut the Velcro strips into 1" pieces.
3. Glue a piece of Velcro, hook side, to one end of a piece of belt.
4. Glue the opposite piece of Velcro, soft side, to the opposite end and underside of the belt.
5. Repeat steps 3 and 4 for each belt piece.
6. Place the belt pieces in the container.

Activity

Show children how to link the pieces of belt together (i.e., attach the Velcro). Encourage children to use descriptive language as they describe the task they are doing (e.g., looping through, making a circle, putting the ends together, and pulling the belts apart). Have children describe the texture of the Velcro and the belts (e.g., rough, smooth, or bumpy). Show children how to unhook the chains and store them in the container when finished.

A Little Something Else

Expand this activity by encouraging children to loop the belts together by size, color, or texture.

Notes

CHOCOLATE CHIPPERS

Instructional Settings

Independent play

Small group (2–5 children)

Skills

Counting with one-to-one correspondence

Recognizing/Identifying numerals to 10

Ordering by number

Describing using senses

Themes

Cookies

Community helpers

Numbers

My neighborhood

Food

Materials

- *Chocolate Chip Cookie Pattern* (see Appendix B, page 182)
- Light-brown heavy stock paper
- Scissors
- Brown fine-point permanent marker
- Empty cookie box

Preparation

1. Duplicate the *Chocolate Chip Cookie Pattern* onto the heavy stock paper to create 22 cookies.
2. Cut out the cookies.
3. On 11 of the cookies, write the numerals 0–10 and the words for 0–10 (i.e., numeral 0 and *zero* on one cookie, numeral 1 and *one* on another, and so on).
4. On the remainder of the cookies, draw 0–10 dots (i.e., one cookie with 0 dots, another cookie with 1 dot, and so on). Shape the dots like chocolate chips.
5. Laminate the cookies.
6. Place the cookies in the cookie box.

Activity

Encourage children to open the box, dump out the cookies, and match the cookies with numerals and words to the cookies with the corresponding number of chocolate chips. Have children arrange the cookies in numerical order. Help children count the cookies and the chocolate chips on the cookies; then identify the numerals. Encourage each child to name his or her favorite kind of cookie and tell why he or she likes it. Graph their favorites. Talk about the person in their community who makes cookies and where in their neighborhood they can buy cookies. Show children how to store the cookies in the cookie box when finished.

A Little Something Else

Expand this activity to include a mixed batch of "real" cookies, which children must sort according to type (e.g., oatmeal, sugar, sandwich, and animal). Make cookies for snack. Encourage children to use the laminated cookies as a prop in the dramatic play center.

Notes

• • •

CLIP IT

Instructional Settings

Independent play
Small group (2–5 children)

Skills

Developing fine-motor coordination
Recognizing/Identifying colors
Recognizing/Identifying full/empty
Matching

Themes

Colors
Numbers
Community helpers

Materials

- Newspaper
- 30 metal hair clips
- Spray paint (the same colors as the bowls)
- 3 small plastic bowls in different colors

Preparation

1. Cover your work area with newspaper.
2. Separate the metal hair clips into 3 groups of 10.
3. Use spray paint to color the metal hair clips (10 hair clips per color).
4. Let the hair clips dry.
5. Turn the hair clips over and paint the other side.
6. Let the hair clips dry.

Activity

Encourage children to name the different colors as they match the colored hair clips to the same colored bowls by either clipping the hair clip to the side of the bowl or dropping the hair clip into the bowl. Encourage children to name the colors. Have children tell if the bowls are full or empty. Show children how to store the clips in the bowls when finished.

A Little Something Else

Encourage children to look around the room and find additional colored items that would fit in the bowls. Have children talk about which community helper would use the hair clips and what the hair clips can be used for.

Notes

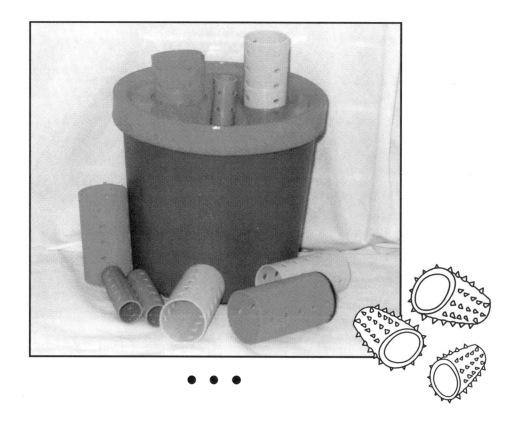

• • •

CURLER CUTOUTS

Instructional Setting

Independent play

Skills

Sorting
Developing fine-motor coordination
Naming objects and their functions
Naming objects by category
Discriminating size, shape, texture
Recognizing/Identifying sizes

Themes

Community helpers
My neighborhood

Materials

- Round plastic container with large top (e.g., ice cream bucket or 5-lb. coffee can)
- Contac paper
- 4 small, 4 medium, and 4 large plastic curlers (available at beauty supply stores; make sure that the diameters vary in size)
- Permanent marker
- Exacto knife

Preparation

1. Cover the lid of the plastic container with the Contac paper.
2. Trace one small, one medium, and one large curler on the top of the container. Make sure that there is plenty of space between the curlers.
3. Cut out the curler shapes.
4. Place the curlers in the container.

Activity

Tell each child to dump the curlers from the container and then place the lid back on. Have each child sort the curlers according to size and then put them in the appropriate holes. Encourage each child to identify the different sizes of curlers (i.e., small, medium, and large). Talk about the place you might find curlers, the community helpers who might use them, and what curlers are used for. Show each child how to store the curlers in the container when finished.

A Little Something Else

Make this activity more challenging by using a larger variety of curler sizes.

Notes

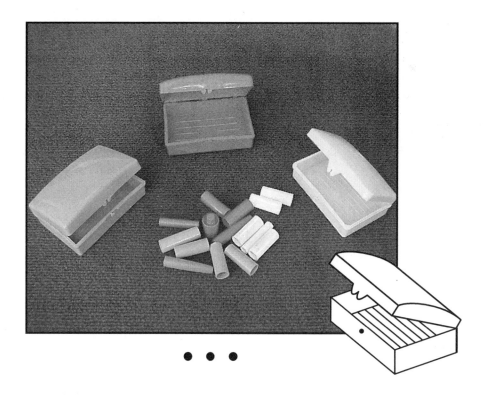

DISH IT UP

Instructional Settings

Independent play

Small group (2–5 children)

Skills

Matching

Recognizing/Identifying colors

Developing fine-motor coordination

Themes

Colors

Numbers

Health

Materials

- 1 red, 1 green, 1 blue, and 1 yellow plastic travel soap dish (available at most Dollar Stores)
- Tops from old red, green, blue, and yellow markers (three or more of each color)
- Container

Preparation

Place all soap dishes and markers in the container.

Activity

Show children how to match the colored marker tops to the corresponding colored soap dish and place the maker tops in the soap dish. Have children name the colors. Talk about how washing your hands helps keep you healthy. Show children how to store the soap dishes and the marker tips in the container when finished.

A Little Something Else

Write a numeral on each soap dish. Show children how to put the corresponding number of marker tops in the soap dishes.

Notes

DONUT MATCH

Instructional Settings

Independent play

Small group (2–5 children)

Skills

Counting with one-to-one correspondence

Matching

Recognizing/Identifying colors

Describing using senses

Naming objects by category

Recognizing/Identifying same/different

Themes

Community helpers

Food

My neighborhood

Colors

Numbers

Materials

- *Donut Pattern* (see Appendix B, page 183)
- Heavy stock paper
- Watercolor markers
- Scissors
- Donut container (available free from most bakeries)
- Clear Contac paper

Preparation

1. Duplicate the *Donut Pattern* onto heavy stock paper to create 20 donuts.
2. Create matching pairs of donuts using colors to represent flavors, such as the following: chocolate frosting, vanilla frosting with blue sprinkles, pink frosting, yellow frosting, yellow frosting with brown sprinkles, no frosting (plain), blue frosting, blue frosting with purple sprinkles, and red frosting.
3. Cut out the donuts and donut "holes."
4. Laminate the donuts and donut holes.

Activity

Show children how to find donuts that match. Help them use the terms *same* and *different* while they look for matches. Have children describe the decorations on the donuts and name the colors and the flavors. Then help them count the pairs of matching donuts. Talk about where you would buy donuts and who makes them. Show children how to store the donuts in the donut container when finished.

A Little Something Else

Using the plates from the *Mac and Cheese Please* activity (see pages 70–71), have children "serve" the same number of donuts as the numeral on the plate. Encourage children to use the donuts as a prop in the dramatic play center.

Notes

DO YOU HEAR WHAT I HEAR?

Instructional Settings

Independent play
Small group (2–5 children)

Skills

Describing using senses
Recognizing/Identifying same/different
Predicting
Matching
Listening

Themes

Senses
Outside/Inside

Materials

- 8–10 unused large plastic medicine bottles with lids (available free from most pharmacies)
- Variety of items (e.g., rice, sand, bells, beans, small rocks, small metal paper clips, flour, cotton balls, sugar, clean cat litter, and pennies)

Preparation

1. Create pairs of medicine bottles by filling them with the same objects (be sure to add the same amount, so the bottles make the same sound).
2. Secure the lids on the bottles.

Activity

Have children shake the bottles and listen to their sounds to find the sounds that match. As children listen to the different sounds, have them talk about each sound using descriptive words. Help them decide if the bottles sound the same or different. Have them predict what is in each bottle.

A Little Something Else

Encourage children to find objects in the classroom that make sounds. Go for a walk outside, and find items from nature that make sounds.

Notes

DREAMERS

Instructional Settings

Independent play

Small group (2–5 children)

Skills

Developing fine-motor coordination

Determining cause and effect

Recognizing/Identifying slow/fast

Predicting

Describing using senses

Themes

Holidays

Water fun

Seasons

Materials

- Sturdy, smooth plastic bottle
- Light corn syrup
- Food coloring
- Glitter or sequins
- Super glue

Preparation

1. Clean and dry the bottle thoroughly.
2. Fill the bottle approximately two-thirds full with light corn syrup.
3. Add several drops of food coloring to the syrup.
4. Add glitter or sequins.
5. Glue the lid on the bottle.

Activity

Have children watch the syrup flow in the bottle. Discuss with children why the syrup and the glitter or sequins move so slowly. Ask children to think of words to describe the movement. Ask them to think about what would happen if the bottle contained water rather than syrup.

A Little Something Else

Make a second bottle with water, food coloring, and glitter or sequins. Discuss with children how the two bottles are the same and how they are different: the water moves fast, the syrup moves slow, the water has bubbles, the syrup has bubbles, and so on. You can make additional bottles at different times of year by adding holiday or seasonal glitter (available at most craft stores) and appropriate food coloring for that holiday or season (e.g., orange food coloring and black bat sequins for Halloween).

Notes

ERASER MATCH

Instructional Setting

Independent play

Skills

Matching

Developing fine-motor coordination

Naming objects and their functions

Discriminating size, shape, texture

Recognizing/Identifying same/different

Themes

Shapes

School

Numbers

Multiple themes

Materials

- Velcro (available at fabric stores)
- Hot glue gun
- 6 unused small plastic medicine bottles (available free from most pharmacies)
- 6 different types of children's novelty erasers (4 of each type; available at teacher supply stores)
- Small bowl

Preparation

1. Glue a small strip of Velcro, soft side, on the side of each plastic bottle.
2. Glue a small strip of Velcro, hook side, on one of each type of eraser.
3. Attach the 6 erasers to the 6 plastic bottles.
4. Place the erasers and the bottles in the small bowl.

Activity

Have each child empty the bowl, and place the erasers in the bottles that have matching erasers. Encourage each child to talk about the shape of each type of eraser and describe what he or she might do with an eraser. Let each child talk about same and different erasers. Show each child how to place the items back in the bowl when finished.

A Little Something Else

Make this game more difficult by placing cards with the numerals 0–5 in front of the container. Have children count out the same number of erasers and drop them in the bottle. Change the erasers often to spark each child's interests and accommodate different themes (e.g., use bears, lions, monkeys, snakes, and tigers when studying zoos).

Notes

FABRIC MATCH

Instructional Settings

Independent play
Small group (2–5 children)

Skills

Matching
Discriminating size, shape, texture
Recognizing/Identifying textures
Recognizing/Identifying same/different
Recognizing/Identifying shapes
Naming objects and their functions
Describing using senses

Themes

Senses
Clothing
Community helpers
Shapes

Materials

- Scissors
- Variety of fabrics (e.g., satin, corduroy, cotton, and fleece) with different colors, designs, and textures

Preparation

1. Cut each piece of fabric into 2, 4" × 4" squares
2. Sew a seam around the edges, so the material does not fray.

Activity

Show children how to match the fabric squares. Talk about the concepts of same and different. Encourage the use of descriptive words by having children feel the different fabrics and talk about them using words (e.g., *smooth, rough, bumpy, soft, stripes, polka dots, plaid,* and *shiny*). Talk about which community helper might use material to sew and what else the materials might be used for.

A Little Something Else

Have children work in pairs with their backs to each other and the fabric squares in their laps. Or the children could sit with the fold and play prop (see pages 140–141) between them. Have one child pick up a piece of fabric, describe it to his or her partner, and put it in front of himself or herself. Have the other child pick out the same fabric square and put it in front of himself or herself. After children place about 5 or 6 fabric squares in a row in front of themselves, have them compare their rows to see if they are the same.

Notes

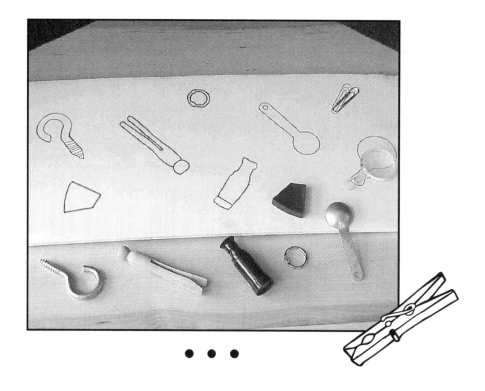

GADGET MATCH

Instructional Settings

Independent play

Small group (2–5 children)

Skills

Matching

Discriminating size, shape, texture

Naming objects and their functions

Developing fine-motor coordination

Themes

Shapes

Multiple themes

Materials

- 6–8 gadgets (e.g., block, round clothespin, teaspoon, spool, large paper clip, wheel from a toy truck, small rattle, and key)
- 11" × 17" poster board or scraps of foam core
- Fine-point permanent marker
- Container

Preparation

1. Place all the gadgets on the poster board or foam core with plenty of space around each object.
2. Trace around each object.
3. Laminate the poster board.
4. Place the gadgets in the container.

Activity

Have children choose a gadget from the container and match the gadget with its corresponding outline. Then have them name the gadgets and tell what they are used for (e.g., a block is for building, a clothespin is for hanging clothes, and a key is for driving a car). Show children how to return the gadgets to the container when finished.

A Little Something Else

Make additional gadget boards using gadgets related to themes or units you may be studying. For example, a small rake, a small shovel, and a small gardening glove could be used for a plant or gardening theme.

Notes

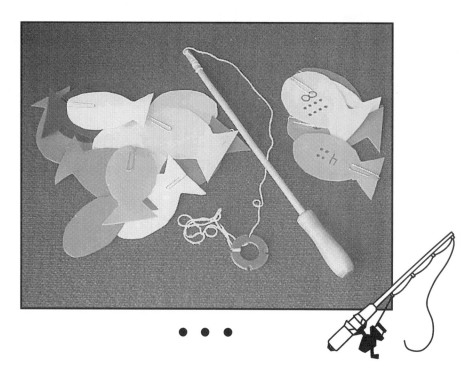

• • •

GONE FISHIN'

Instructional Settings

Independent play

Small group (2–5 children)

Skills

Developing fine-motor coordination

Recognizing/Identifying colors

Naming objects by category

Themes

Colors

Ponds

Letters

Numbers

Water fun

Shapes

Materials

- *Fish Pattern* (see Appendix B, page 184)
- Heavy stock paper
- Scissors
- Fine-point permanent marker
- Craft foam in a variety of colors (available at craft stores)
- Large paper clips
- Empty bucket or small wading pool
- String
- 2–3' stick (e.g., thin branch from a tree or broom handle)
- Strong circular magnet (available at hardware stores)

Preparation

1. Duplicate the *Fish Pattern* onto heavy stock paper.
2. Cut out the fish and use it as a template.
3. Trace the fish on a variety of colors of craft foam and cut them out.
4. Attach a paper clip to each fish.
5. Place the fish in the bucket or the wading pool.
6. Tie the string to one end of the stick (fishing pole).
7. Tie the magnet to the opposite end of the string.

Activity

Have children drop the fishing line into the bucket or wading pool, pull a fish out, and name the color of the fish. Talk about where you might catch fish, and have children name the types of fish they know.

A Little Something Else

Expand this activity by writing numerals, letters, or shapes on the fish using a permanent marker.

Notes

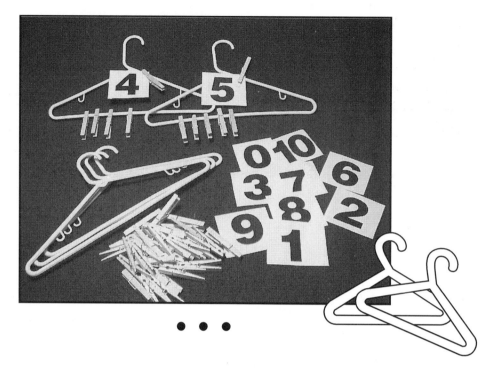

• • •

HANG IT HERE

Instructional Settings

Independent play

Small group (2–5 children)

Skills

Recognizing/Identifying numerals to 10

Developing fine-motor coordination

Counting with one-to-one correspondence

Naming objects and their functions

Ordering by number

Themes

Numbers

Clothing

Colors

Community helpers

Materials

- *Numerals 0–5* (see Appendix B, page 185)
- *Numerals 6–10* (see Appendix B, page 186)
- Heavy stock paper
- Scissors
- 10 plastic coat hangers
- Clear, wide packing tape
- 55–65 wooden clothespins
- Bowl

Preparation

1. Duplicate *Numerals 0–5* and *Numerals 6–10* onto heavy stock paper.
2. Cut the cards apart and laminate them.
3. Place a card at the top of each hanger and secure it in place with the tape or a clothespin.
4. Place the clothespins in the bowl.

Activity

Show children how to look at the numeral and then hang the appropriate number of clothespins on the hanger. Have children identify the numerals and order the hangers by number. Then talk about who cleans clothes and how clothespins and hangers are used. Show children how to take the clothespins off the hangers and store them in the bowl when finished.

A Little Something Else

Expand this activity to include color matching. Provide blank colored index cards. Color the wooden clothespins with markers or paint or substitute colored plastic clothespins for the wooden clothespins. If desired, add dots to the cards to represent the numerals, add number words to the cards, or add both.

Notes

HANG IT UP

Instructional Settings

Independent play

Small group (2–5 children)

Themes

Numbers

Colors

Skills

Counting with one-to-one correspondence

Recognizing/Identifying numerals to 5

Ordering by number

Materials

- *Numerals 0–5* (see Appendix B, page 185)
- Heavy stock paper
- Scissors
- 6 shower curtain hooks
- 15 macrame-type beads (available at craft stores)

Preparation

1. Duplicate *Numerals 0–5* onto heavy stock paper.
2. Cut the cards apart and laminate them.
3. Open one shower curtain hook, slip one bead on it, and close the hook.
4. Continue with the other shower curtain hooks, slipping 2 beads on one, 3 beads on another, 4 beads on another, and finally 5 beads on a hook. One hook will have no beads on it.

Activity

Have children count the beads and match the appropriate shower curtain hook and beads with the numeral card. Have children identify the numerals. Encourage children to put the hooks in number order.

A Little Something Else

Expand this activity to include color matching. Place the same color beads on each hook (e.g., one blue bead, two red beads, three green beads, four yellow beads, and five orange beads). Use the same color markers to trace over the numerals on the numeral cards. If desired, add dots to the cards to represent the numerals, add number words to the cards, or add both.

Notes

HAPPY BIRTHDAY

Instructional Setting

Independent play

Skills

Developing fine-motor coordination
Counting with one-to-one correspondence
Ordering by number
Recognizing/Identifying numerals to 10
Describing feelings

Themes

Celebrations
I'm me
Numbers
Feelings
Boxes and bows

Materials

- 11 empty small plastic margarine or butter tubs with lids that are free of design or writing
- 55 golf tees
- Sandpaper (medium grit)
- Hole punch
- Permanent marker
- Variety of children's birthday cards with a number (from 1 through 10) on the front of each card and one card with no number on the front (to represent 0)
- Box wrapped in birthday wrapping paper

Preparation

1. Clean and dry the plastic tubs and lids.
2. Sand the points of the golf tees until smooth and flat.
3. Punch holes along the entire inside edge of each lid.
4. Draw a birthday cake on each lid.
5. Place the golf tees in several of the tubs and put the tubs and the birthday cards in the box.

Activity

Tell each child to place all the birthday cards in a pile, upside down on the table in front of himself or herself. Have each child pick the top card, look at the number (if present) on the card, and place that number of golf tees (i.e., candles) in the cake (i.e., the lid). Help each child put the lids in number order and identify each numeral. Have each child tell you about his or her birthday. Encourage the use of descriptive words as each child discusses his or her feelings associated with birthdays. Show each child how to store the golf tees in one of the plastic tubs and put the tubs and cards in the birthday box when finished.

A Little Something Else

Provide children with small squares of Styrofoam and a small plastic hammer. Show children how to hammer the golf tees into the Styrofoam.

Notes

HIDE AND SEEK

Instructional Settings

Independent play
Small group (2–5 children)

Skills

Matching
Discriminating size, shape, texture
Naming objects and their functions

Themes

Light and dark
Shapes

Materials

- 6–8 small white objects (e.g., toddler sock, comb, plastic spoon, small baby bottle without the nipple, ruler, stuffed bear)
- White sheet of paper
- Scissors
- 8½" × 11" heavy stock paper
- Rubber cement

Preparation

1. Photocopy each item by setting the copier to the darkest setting and placing a white piece of paper behind the item.
2. Cut out the images.
3. Glue the shapes on the heavy stock paper.
4. Laminate each piece of heavy stock paper.

Activity

Have children name each object and match it to its "shadow" by placing the object on top of its picture. Ask children to tell what each object does.

A Little Something Else

Take children outside to see how the sun casts shadows. Talk about how the sun creates a shadow. Trace around each child's shadow with chalk.

Notes

JINGLE POCKET

Instructional Settings

Independent play

Small group (2–5 children)

Themes

Senses

Holidays

Skills

Counting with one-to-one correspondence

Recognizing/Identifying numerals to 10

Predicting

Discriminating size, shape, texture

Materials

- Scissors
- Fabric
- Permanent marker
- 55 small bells (approximately 2"; available at craft or fabric stores)

Preparation

1. Cut the fabric into 22, 6" × 6" squares; sort squares to make 11 pairs.
2. To form a jingle pocket, sew each pair of fabric squares together, leaving approximately a 3" opening on one end.
3. Write the numeral 1 on the first pocket. If desired, write *Feel Me, How Many Bells?* on each pocket (on the side that does not contain the numeral).
4. Place one bell inside the pocket.
5. Sew the hole shut.
6. Continue with the remaining pockets, writing a numeral on a fabric square, placing that many bells in each pocket, and sewing the pocket shut.
7. Write the numeral 0 on the last pocket and sew it shut.

Activity

Have children look at the numeral on the pocket and feel and count the bells inside. For children who need more of a challenge, place the jingle pockets on a table with the number side down. Have children feel the bells in the pockets and guess how many are in each. Show children how to check their answer by turning the pocket over and looking at the numeral. Encourage children to identify the shape of the bells and predict when they might hear jingle bells.

A Little Something Else

Add the jingle pockets to the music center as a prop.

Notes

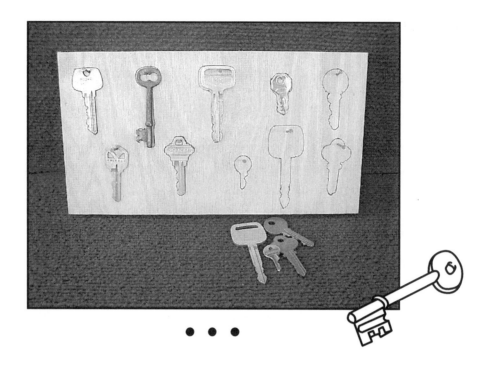

THE KEY TO IT ALL

Instructional Settings

Independent play

Small group (2–5 children)

Skills

Developing fine-motor coordination

Matching

Discriminating size, shape, texture

Naming objects and their functions

Themes

Transportation

Community helpers

Materials

- Sandpaper (heavy grit)
- 1" × 6" × 12" wooden board
- Hammer
- Nails
- Ruler
- Variety of keys (available free from most hardware stores, locksmiths, or key shops that discard improperly cut keys)
- Fine-point permanent marker

Preparation

1. Sand the edges of the board until smooth.
2. Hammer nails at approximately 2" intervals in two rows or in a straight line along the top of the board.
3. Place a key on the first nail and trace around the outside of the key and the inside of the keyhole.
4. Continue with the remaining keys.

Activity

Encourage children to match the keys to the outline of the key on the board. Have children talk about how people use keys and then name different community helpers who might use keys regularly in their jobs (e.g., bus driver, taxi driver, and store owner).

A Little Something Else

Substitute large plastic keys from an infant's teething ring for the small keys and eliminate the board and nails. Trace the keys on a poster board. Have children match the key with the outline of the key.

Notes

• • •

LADYBUG, LADYBUG, FLY AWAY HOME

Instructional Settings

Independent play

Small group (2–5 children)

Skills

Counting with one-to-one correspondence

Naming objects by category

Recognizing/Identifying numerals to 10

Ordering by number

Recognizing/Identifying more/less

Themes

Insects

Gardening

Outside/Inside

Seasons

Flowers

Numbers

Materials

- *Ladybug Patterns* (see Appendix B, page 187)
- *Leaf Pattern* (see Appendix B, page 188)
- Heavy stock paper
- Scissors
- Green, red, and black craft foam (available at craft stores)
- Hot glue gun
- Black fine-point permanent marker

Preparation

1. Duplicate the *Ladybug Patterns* and the *Leaf Pattern* onto heavy stock paper.
2. Cut out the patterns to use as templates.
3. Trace and cut out 10 ladybug bodies from the black foam.
4. Trace and cut out 10 ladybug wings from the red foam.
5. Hot glue a red wing to each black body.
6. Draw 1–10 dots on the ladybug wings (i.e., 1 dot on one wing, 2 dots on another, and so on).
7. Trace and cut out 10 leaf shapes from the green foam.
8. Write the numerals 1–10 on the leaves (i.e., numeral 1 on one leaf, numeral 2 on another, and so on).

Activity

Show children how to match the ladybugs with the dots to the corresponding numerals on the leaves. Then have them count the ladybugs or leaves and arrange them in number order. Talk about which ladybugs have more spots and which have less. Have children name other insects.

A Little Something Else

Bring in live ladybugs for children to observe. Talk about how ladybugs are helpful to gardens (e.g., they eat aphids).

Notes

MAC AND CHEESE PLEASE

Instructional Settings

Independent play

Small group (2–5 children)

Skills

Counting with one-to-one correspondence

Developing fine-motor coordination

Recognizing/Identifying numerals to 10

Ordering by number

Recognizing/Identifying more/less

Describing feelings

Themes

Numbers

Boxes and bows

Food

Feelings

Materials

- Orange food coloring (mix yellow and red)
- Rubbing alcohol
- Large bowl with tight fitting lid
- Uncooked macaroni
- Paper towels
- Empty macaroni and cheese box
- Clear Contac paper
- Permanent marker
- 11 large paper plates
- Large plastic zipper bag
- Small spoon

Preparation

1. Mix the orange food coloring with ⅛ cup of the rubbing alcohol in the large bowl.
2. Add the uncooked macaroni to the large bowl, put the lid on, and shake to mix.
3. Remove the macaroni and lay it on paper towels to dry.
4. Cover the empty box of macaroni and cheese box with clear Contac paper.
5. Write the numerals 0–10 and the words for 0–10 on the paper plates (i.e., numeral 0 and *zero* on one plate, numeral 1 and *one* another, and so on).
6. Place the macaroni in the large plastic zipper bag when it has dried and place the bag in the empty macaroni and cheese box.

Activity

Have children open the bag and spoon out the same number of scoops of macaroni and cheese as the numeral on the plate. Have children count the number of plates. Encourage them to discuss if there is more or less macaroni on the different plates. Then have them put the plates in numerical order. Tell children to describe how they feel about eating macaroni and cheese. Show children how to put the macaroni and cheese in the plastic zipper bag and store it in the macaroni and cheese box when finished.

A Little Something Else

Make macaroni and cheese for snack, and have children count as they scoop the macaroni onto their plate.

McFRIES

Instructional Settings

Independent play

Small group (2–5 children)

Skills

Counting with one-to-one correspondence

Recognizing/Identifying numerals to 10

Ordering by number

Developing fine-motor coordination

Naming objects by category

Themes

Numbers

Gardening

My neighborhood

Food

Materials

- Scissors
- Red and light-brown felt (available at craft stores)
- Permanent marker or fabric paint
- Cardboard French fry container (available free from most fast-food restaurants)

Preparation

1. Cut 11 ketchup splashes (approximately 3½" × 2½") out of the red felt.
2. Cut 55 French fries (3½" × ½") out of the brown felt.
3. Label the ketchup splashes with the numerals 0–10 (i.e., numeral 0 on one ketchup splash, numeral 1 on another, and so on). Add the numeral words *zero, one,* and so on to each ketchup splash if desired.
4. Add dots corresponding to the numerals to the back of the ketchup splashes, so children can self-check their work.
5. Place the ketchup splashes and the French fries in the French fry container.

Activity

Have children place the ketchup splashes in correct numerical order and count the ketchup splashes. Show children how to count the correct number of French fries and match them with the ketchup splash with the same numeral. Talk about other foods available at a fast-food restaurant in their neighborhood. Show children how to store the French fries and the ketchup splashes in the French fry container when finished.

A Little Something Else

Have French fries for snack. Place toothpicks in a potato, and immerse half the potato in water to show how a potato will root and sprout. Encourage children to use the felt French fries as a prop in the dramatic center.

Notes

• • •

MAKING FACES

Instructional Settings

Independent play

Small group (2–5 children)

Skills

Developing fine-motor coordination

Describing feelings

Developing self-awareness

Naming objects and their functions

Themes

I'm me

Body parts

Feelings

Farm animals

Senses

Materials

- Variety of close-up photographs of children's faces (e.g., magazine pictures or class photos)
- Poster board
- Scissors
- Velcro strips with adhesive backing (available at fabric stores)
- Ruler
- Black marker
- Unused pizza box (available free from most pizza places)
- Hot glue gun
- Velcro sensitive fabric (available at fabric stores) or headliner fabric (scraps available free from most auto upholstery shops that install headliner)
- Yarn

Preparation

1. Glue each photo onto the poster board.
2. Cut apart each photo, separating the eyes, nose, mouth, and ears; laminate the pieces.
3. Place a small piece of the Velcro, hook side, on the back of each facial feature
4. Cut the Velcro sensitive or headliner fabric to fit in the pizza box top. Then cut it into four equal pieces. Glue each piece inside the pizza box top.
5. Label each section with the following: *Eyes, Nose, Mouth,* and *Ears.*
6. Stick facial feature pieces on the appropriate sections.
7. Cut the Velcro sensitive or headliner fabric into an oval shape that fits inside the pizza box; this will be the "face." Glue the oval to the bottom of the pizza box and glue the yarn at the top of the oval to represent hair.

Activity

Have children explore the various facial features by placing them in the appropriate places on the face or making silly faces and placing the features in unconventional places on the face. Have children name the facial features and tell what each feature does. Encourage children to discuss feelings and emotions demonstrated by the mouths. Show children where the eyes, ears, nose, and mouth can be stored (on the box top) when finished.

A Little Something Else

Expand this activity to use pictures of animals that are familiar to the children, including pets, zoo animals, creatures from the sea, and farm animals.

McNUGGET MUNCH

Instructional Settings

Independent play

Small group (2–5 children)

Skills

Counting with one-to-one correspondence

Recognizing/Identifying numerals to 10

Ordering by number

Naming objects by category

Describing using senses

Themes

Numbers

My neighborhood

Food

Materials

- *Oval Shapes* (see Appendix B, page 189)
- Heavy stock paper
- Scissors
- Light-brown felt (available at craft stores)
- Brown permanent marker or fabric paint
- Cardboard chicken nugget box (available free from most fast-food restaurants)

Preparation

1. Duplicate *Oval Shapes* onto heavy stock paper.
2. Cut out 1 oval to use as a tracing template.
3. Trace 22 ovals (nuggets) onto the light-brown felt.
4. On 11 nuggets, write the numerals 0–10 (i.e., numeral 0 on one nugget, numeral 1 on another, and so on).
5. For the remaining 11 nuggets, cut 0–10 small holes (bites) (i.e., 0 holes in one nugget, 1 hole in another, and so on).
6. Place the nuggets in the chicken nugget box.

Activity

Encourage children to count the number of bites in the nuggets and match the nuggets with numerals to the nuggets with the bites. Have children put the chicken nuggets in numerical order. Ask children to talk about when they have had chicken nuggets and how they tasted. Also talk about where they can buy chicken nuggets and other warm snacks. Show children how to store the nuggets in the nugget box when finished.

A Little Something Else

Cook chicken nuggets for snack. Encourage children to use the felt nuggets as props in the dramatic center.

Notes

MIRROR MAGIC

Instructional Settings

Independent play

Small group (2–5 children)

Skills

Describing using senses

Predicting

Recognizing/Identifying same/different

Developing self-awareness

Recognizing/Identifying colors

Recognizing/Identifying shapes

Themes

I'm me

Shapes

Colors

Body parts

Materials

- Hot glue gun or masking tape
- Small unbreakable mirrors (available at craft stores)
- *Mirror Images* (see Appendix B, page 190–192)
- Heavy stock paper
- Scissors
- Watercolor markers

Preparation

1. Place a strip of glue or a strip of tape around the edge of each mirror, so the edges are smooth.
2. Duplicate *Mirror Images* onto heavy stock paper and cut the images apart.
3. Color the pictures, so each half of the card is different, for example:
   Tree—color the trunk and branches brown and the leaves green.
   Ice cream—color the ice cream brown for chocolate.
   Boy—color the curly hair red, the straight hair black, one eye green, and one eye blue.
   Girl—color the braid yellow, the hair brown, one eye green, and one eye blue.
   Apple—color the apple red but keep the bite white.
   Clown—color half the hair orange and half purple, half the mouth pink and half yellow, one eye blue, and one eye green.
4. Laminate the cards.

Activity

Tell children to place the cards in front of themselves. Have children predict what image will appear in the mirror if they place a mirror in the middle of a picture. Show children how to hold the mirror in the middle of one of the pictures. Have children describe the images with and without the mirror, talking about colors and shapes and using the words *same* and *different*. Have each child look in the mirror and discuss what he or she sees. Ask questions, such as "What color are your eyes?" "Can you see your whole face?" "What do you see behind you?"

A Little Something Else

Have children experiment on other pictures in the classroom using the mirror.

MMMM! GINGERBREAD

Instructional Setting

Independent play

Skills

Developing fine-motor coordination

Counting with one-to-one correspondence

Recognizing/Identifying numerals to 10

Recognizing/Identifying colors

Ordering by number

Recognizing/Identifying more/less

Themes

Food

Colors

Cookies

Holidays

Numbers

Materials

- *Gingerbread Pattern* (see Appendix B, page 193)
- Heavy stock paper
- Watercolor markers
- Scissors
- Paper or plastic plates
- Cookie sheet
- Spatula

Preparation

1. Duplicate the *Gingerbread Pattern* onto heavy stock paper to create 10 gingerbread people.
2. Draw and color 1–10 buttons on the fronts of the gingerbread people (i.e., 1 button on one gingerbread person, 2 buttons on another, and so on). (As an option, cut gingerbread people out of craft foam and glue on buttons using a hot glue gun.)
3. Cut out the gingerbread people and laminate them.
4. Write the numerals 1–10 on the paper or plastic plates (i.e., numeral 1 on one plate, numeral 2 on another, and so on).

Activity

Have each child put the plates in front of himself or herself and place the gingerbread people on the cookie sheet. Show each child how to count the buttons on a gingerbread person and then match the number of buttons to the plate with the same numeral. Show each child how to lift the gingerbread person off the cookie sheet with the spatula and place it on the plate. Encourage each child to count the gingerbread people. Have each child identify the colors of the buttons. Then help each child put the plates in numerical order. Talk about the concepts of more and less regarding the gingerbread people's buttons.

A Little Something Else

Make gingerbread cookies for snack, and encourage children to decorate their cookies with icing and small candies. Suggest that children use the laminated gingerbread people as props in the dramatic play center.

Notes

• • •

NAME/PICTURE MATCH

Instructional Settings

Independent play
Small group (2–5 children)

Skills

Matching
Discriminating size, shape, texture
Developing self-awareness
Naming objects and their functions
Developing fine-motor coordination
Recognizing/Identifying words

Themes

I'm me
School
Friends
Multiple themes

Materials

- Glue
- Photo of each child in class
- 8½" × 11" heavy stock paper
- Fine-point permanent marker
- Scissors

Preparation

1. Glue a child's picture on the left side of a sheet of heavy stock paper.
2. Write that child's name on the right side of the sheet of heavy stock paper.
3. Cut a squiggly or jagged line between the picture and the child's name to create a unique puzzle for each child.
4. Laminate all the pieces.

Activity

Have children assemble the puzzles by matching each photo with the corresponding child's name. Have children name the pictures on the cards, including themselves.

A Little Something Else

This activity can be expanded to include multiple themes. For example, pictures of family members, pictures of adult and baby animals, upper- and lowercase letters, or numerals and number sets.

Notes

OUTSIDE/INSIDE

Instructional Settings

Independent play
Small group (2–5 children)

Skills

Naming objects and their functions
Matching
Naming objects by category
Recognizing/Identifying words
Describing feelings

Themes

Outside/Inside
Weather
Seasons

Materials

- Black permanent marker
- Several sheets of 8½" × 11" heavy stock paper or poster board
- Photographs of people, places, activities, or objects found indoors (e.g., people eating, person washing dishes, person working at a desk, child watching TV, table, bed, and bathtub)
- Glue
- Photographs of people, places, activities, or objects found outdoors (e.g., swing set, lake, people skiing, playground, people playing soccer, tree house, and people camping)

Preparation

1. Write the word *Outside* on a sheet of heavy stock paper or poster board and glue an "outside" picture on the paper.
2. Write the word *Inside* on a sheet of heavy stock paper or poster board and glue an "inside" picture on the paper.
3. Glue the rest of the pictures on the remaining heavy stock paper or poster board.
4. Laminate the pictures.

Activity

Have children match the photographs of the outside activities to the "outside" page and the photographs of the inside activities to the "inside" page. Have children name the activities and objects and talk about other outdoor and indoor activities or objects. Ask children to describe what they enjoy doing outdoors and indoors.

A Little Something Else

Encourage children to bring photographs from home to make an outside/inside collage.

Notes

PACK A PENCIL BAG

Instructional Setting

Independent play

Skills

Matching

Sorting

Recognizing/Identifying colors

Naming objects and their functions

Developing fine-motor coordination

Themes

Numbers

School

Colors

Materials

- Blue, green, and red school items, such as:
    - memo books
    - crayons
    - pencils
    - markers
    - erasers
    - colored pencils
    - pencil grips
    - pens
    - school supplies that might be in an art center (e.g., construction paper, colored glue, glitter, and stamp pads)
- Blue, green and red pencil bags (one in each color)
- Container

Preparation

Place all the items, except the pencil bags, in the container.

Activity

Instruct each child to place the school supplies into the pencil bags according to color. Have each child name the colors of the objects. Encourage each child to suggest ways the different school materials would be used at school. Show each child how to store items in the container when finished.

A Little Something Else

Expand this activity to include additional colors or have each child choose a card with a numeral printed on it and put that many colored objects in the bag.

Notes

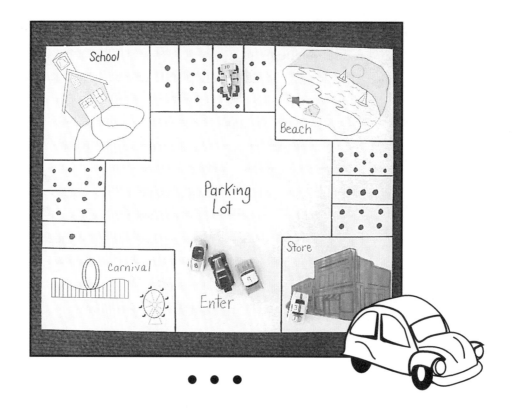

PARK IT HERE

Instructional Settings

Independent play

Small group (2–5 children)

Skills

Developing fine-motor coordination

Counting with one-to-one correspondence

Ordering by number

Recognizing/Identifying numerals to 10

Naming objects by category

Themes

Transportation

Numbers

My neighborhood

Materials

- *Locations* (see Appendix B, page 194)
- Scissors
- Glue
- Poster board
- Fine-point permanent marker
- 10 small toy cars

Preparation

1. Duplicate the *Locations* and cut them apart (or cut pictures from magazines or coloring books of locations that represent the children's neighborhood).
2. Glue a location on each corner of the poster board.
3. Draw "parking" spaces on the left side of the poster board, at the top, and on the right side of the poster board. Add an "entrance" at the bottom of the poster board.
4. Print the words *Parking Lot* in the center of the poster board and *Enter* at the bottom. Label each location.
5. Write the numerals 1–10 on the cars (i.e., numeral 1 on one car, numeral 2 on another, and so on).
6. Number each space with 1–10 dots (i.e., 1 dot on one space, 2 dots on another, and so on).
7. Laminate the poster board.

Activity

Encourage children to first organize the cars in numerical order. Ask children to name different types of cars. Ask them to tell what kind of car their family drives. Then have children drive the cars and match the numerals on the cars to the parking space with the corresponding number of dots.

A Little Something Else

Encourage children to use the cars and the parking lot as props in the block center.

Notes

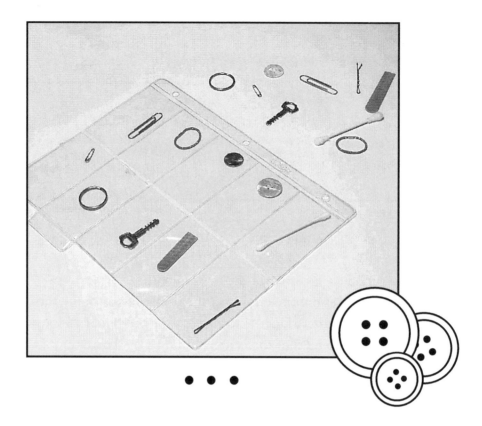

• • •

PICK A POCKET

Instructional Setting

Independent play

Skills

Developing fine-motor coordination

Matching

Discriminating size, shape, texture

Naming objects and their functions

Recognizing/Identifying shapes

Recognizing/Identifying colors

Themes

Colors

Shapes

Multiple themes

Materials

- 8½" × 11" vinyl pocket business card holder (available at most office supply stores)
- Pairs of small items of various shapes that will fit into the business card holder (e.g., paper clips, rubber bands, buttons, and erasers)
- Container

Preparation

1. Slide one item from each pair into each pocket of the business card holder.
2. Place the other item from each pair into the storage container.

Activity

Show each child how to select an object from the container, identify it, and match it to an object in the business card holder. Encourage each child to tell the function of the items in the pockets and describe the shape or color (if appropriate). Show each child how to return the small items to the container when finished.

A Little Something Else

Change the items in the business card holder to represent multiple themes (e.g., for a fall theme, gather yellow leaves, pumpkin seeds, apple seeds, and acorns; for a color theme, gather an assortment of objects in the desired color). To incorporate larger items, use a large vinyl shoe organizer.

Notes

• • •

PLANTING FLOWERS

Instructional Settings

Independent play

Small group (2–5 children)

Skills

Matching

Recognizing/Identifying colors

Naming objects by category

Naming objects and their functions

Developing fine-motor coordination

Describing using senses

Themes

Flowers

Seasons

Colors

Gardening

Outside/Inside

Senses

Materials

- 6 orange juice cans
- 6 different colors of construction paper
- Clear Contac paper
- *Flower Pattern* (see Appendix B, page 195)
- Scissors
- Hot glue gun
- 24 green pipe cleaners

Preparation

1. Wrap each orange juice can with a different color of construction paper.
2. Cover the construction paper with the clear Contac paper.
3. Duplicate the *Flower Pattern* onto 6 different colors of construction paper.
4. Cut 8 identical flower shapes out of the 6 different colors of construction paper for a total of 48 flowers. (An Ellison Die-Cut machine also works well for this but it is not necessary.)
5. Laminate the flowers.
6. Separate the flowers into 24 pairs.
7. Glue the pipe cleaner on one of the flowers and glue another flower on top—do this for the remainder of the flowers (use the same color flower for both sides).

Activity

Show children how to "plant" the flowers by matching the flower color to the same color flowerpot (i.e., the covered juice can). Have children name the different colors and different types of flowers. Encourage children to describe flowers. Ask how flowers smell and discuss where they are found and what they are used for. Show children how to store the flowers in the flowerpots when finished.

A Little Something Else

Bring in real flowers to plant in a garden or in flowerpots. Use 3 different sizes of flowerpots to develop size concepts.

Notes

POPCORN FUN

Instructional Settings

Independent play
Small group (2–5 children)

Skills

Matching
Recognizing/Identifying alphabet letters
Developing sound-symbol correspondence
Naming objects by category

Themes

Letters
Numbers
Food
My neighborhood

Materials

- Scissors
- Yellow felt (available at craft stores)
- Brown and red fine-point permanent marker or red fabric paint
- One small or child's size popcorn bag (available free from most movie theaters)

Preparation

1. Cut the felt into 52, 2" × 2" popcorn-shaped pieces.
2. Trace around each piece using the brown permanent marker or fabric paint.
3. Write all the upper- and lowercase letters of the alphabet on the popcorn pieces (i.e., letter A on one piece, letter a on another, and so on).
4. Place all the popcorn pieces in the popcorn bag.

Activity

Have children dump out all the popcorn. Encourage them to match the popcorn with the lowercase letter to the popcorn with the corresponding uppercase letter. Help children name the letters of the alphabet and the sounds they make. Then talk about where and when children would eat popcorn, and name other activities that go with having popcorn.

A Little Something Else

Expand this activity to include counting with one-to-one correspondence by acquiring 10 popcorn bags and cutting out 55 popcorn shapes. Write the numerals 1–10 on the bags, (i.e., numeral 1 on one bag, numeral 2 on another, and so on) and have children drop the correct number of popcorn pieces in the bags. Include this activity at snack, having children count the popcorn you have popped.

Notes

• • •

PUPPET PALS

Instructional Settings

Independent play
Small group (2–5 children)

Skills

Developing self-awareness
Describing feelings
Naming objects by category
Retelling a story/song/chant

Themes

I'm me
Families
Community helpers
Feelings
Friends

Materials

- Cardboard rolls from toilet paper
- Colored tape or colored Contac paper
- Scissors
- Children's photos
- Glue
- Clear Contac paper

Preparation

1. Cover the toilet paper rolls with the colored tape or colored Contac paper.
2. Cut out the children's photos, so they fit on the rolls.
3. Glue the photos on the rolls.
4. Cover the rolls with clear Contac paper.

Activity

Have children use the puppets in different ways: to recognize themselves, to recognize and name their friends, to tell stories or role-play, and to communicate their feelings.

A Little Something Else

Use the puppets at circle time or at the snack table as seat assignments. Or make community helper puppets using photographs of firefighters, police officers, doctors, teachers, grocers, bus drivers, cashiers, dentists, salespeople, waitpersons, and other members of the community.

Further extend this activity by sending home a letter asking for photographs of family members and making each child a set of "family" puppets. (Remind families that the photos will not be returned.) Have children discuss their families and name the members of their families.

Notes

• • •

SCRUBBER NUMBER

Instructional Setting

Small group (2–5 children)

Skills

Counting with one-to-one correspondence

Ordering by number

Developing fine-motor coordination

Recognizing/Identifying numerals to 10

Naming objects and their functions

Recognizing/Identifying textures

Describing using senses

Themes

Numbers

Senses

Materials

- Deck of cards
- Pink hair picks (available at beauty supply stores)
- Plastic bowl with lid
- 10 scrubber pads (used to clean dishes)

Preparation

1. Remove a 10, 9, 8, 7, 6, 5, 4, 3, and 2 of any suit from the deck of cards.
2. Put the cards and the picks in the bowl and put the lid on.

Activity

Have children open the bowl and remove the contents. Tell them to place the scrubbers in front of themselves on a table and to place the cards upside down, in a pile on the table. Then have children choose a card from the pile and place it in front of one of the scrubbers. Children should stick the same number of picks in the scrubber as the numeral on the card. Have children put the scrubbers in number order based on the number of picks. Help children use descriptive words to describe how the scrubbers feel (rough) versus how the cards feel (smooth). Then ask children what the scrubbers are usually used for. Show children how to return the cards and the picks to the bowl when finished.

A Little Something Else

Adapt this activity for younger children by eliminating the cards and letting children experiment with the picks and the scrubbers. (However, watch children very closely.)

Notes

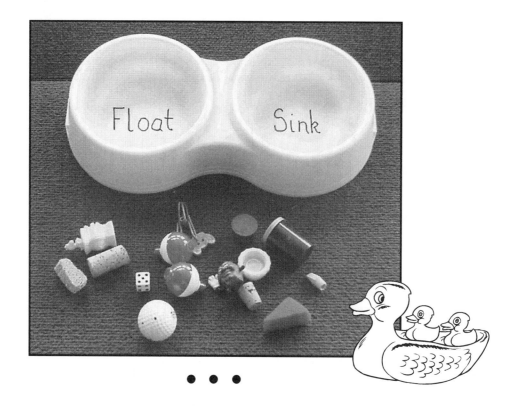

• • •

SINKER AND FLOATER

Instructional Settings

Independent play

Small group (2–5 children)

Large group (6–10 children)

Skills

Developing fine-motor coordination

Determining cause and effect

Sorting

Predicting

Themes

Water fun

Seasons

Ponds

Materials

- Black permanent marker
- Large pet dish with 2 compartments (available at pet stores)
- Water
- Small items that sink (e.g., penny, rock, and marble)
- Small items that float (e.g., fishing bobber, sponge, and cork)
- Basket or box

Preparation

1. Write *Float* in one compartment of the pet dish and *Sink* in the other compartment.
2. Fill the compartments half full with water.

Activity

Have children lay the items on the table in front of them and predict whether they will sink or float. They can sort the items into groups of sink and float as they make their decisions. Then they can place the items in the compartments of water to see if they sink or float. Discuss with children which items float and which items sink and why. Show children how to store the items in the basket or box when finished.

A Little Something Else

For younger children, use large items in a water table or in a small wading pool.

Notes

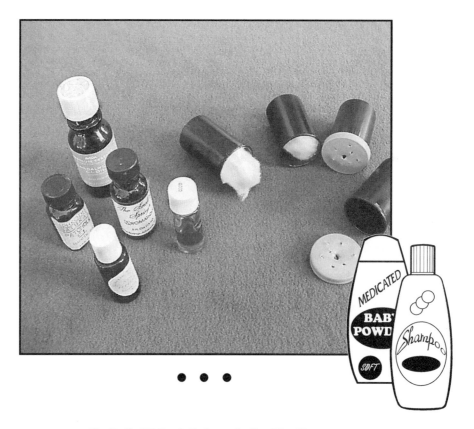

• • •

SMELLY JARS

Instructional Settings

Independent play

Small group (2–5 children)

Skills

Predicting

Matching

Describing using senses

Recognizing/Identifying same/different

Describing feelings

Themes

Senses

Flowers

Feelings

Materials

- Cotton balls
- Variety of scents (e.g., peppermint oil, perfume, vanilla, spices, bath oils, baby powder, shampoo, coffee, grape juice, tea, and dry cocoa mix)
- 8–10 plastic film canisters and lids (available free from most camera stores or drugstores where film is processed on-site)
- Awl, ice pick, or other sharp tool

Preparation

1. Saturate 2 cotton balls with the same scent.
2. Place each cotton ball in a film canister.
3. Continue with other scents until you have 4 or 5 pairs of scents.
4. Secure the lids on the canisters. (Resaturate the cotton balls periodically as needed.)
5. Punch a few small holes in the lids of the canisters. (Do not leave the sharp tool in an area where children can get to it.)

Activity

Tell children there are two canisters with the same scent. Then encourage them to sniff the different scents and match the ones that smell the same. If the smells are not the same, encourage them to use the word *different*. Have them predict what might be making the smell and describe how they like the scent. Chart the children's likes and dislikes.

A Little Something Else

Collect the label from the container of each scent used in this activity. Glue the labels on note cards. Laminate the note cards or cover them with clear Contac paper. Review with children the different scents and the matching labels. Have children match each scent to the correct label.

Notes

• • •

SOAP IT UP

Instructional Settings

Independent play

Small group (2–5 children)

Skills

Matching

Recognizing/Identifying colors

Describing using senses

Themes

Colors

Health

Letters

Numbers

I'm me

Materials

- *Oval Shapes* (see Appendix B, page 189)
- Heavy stock paper
- Empty box from a bar of soap
- Watercolor markers
- Black permanent marker
- Scissors
- Clear Contac paper
- Bar of soap

Preparation

1. Duplicate *Oval Shapes* onto heavy stock paper to create 16 shapes that resemble bars of soap. Make sure the oval shapes will fit in the empty box of soap.
2. Color 2 bars of soap in each of the following colors: red, green, blue, pink, yellow, orange, and purple; leave 2 bars of soap white.
3. Write the corresponding color word on each bar of soap.
4. Cut out the bars of soap and laminate them.
5. Cover the soap box with clear Contac paper.
6. Rub the laminated bars of soap with the real bar of soap to give them a soapy smell.

Activity

Have children match the bars of soap by color. Ask children to name the colors of the soap. Encourage children to describe how the soap smells and talk about how important it is to use soap to stay clean and ward off germs. Show children how to store the soap in the box when finished.

A Little Something Else

Expand this activity to include matching letters, numerals, photographs, or names.

Notes

SOCK IT TO ME

Instructional Settings

Independent play

Small group (2–5 children)

Large group (6–10 children)

Skills

Matching

Sorting

Counting with one-to-one correspondence

Discriminating size, shape, texture

Describing using senses

Recognizing/Identifying textures

Themes

Clothing

Colors

Body parts

Materials

- Several pairs of socks in a variety of sizes, colors, textures, and designs
- Clear plastic shoebox

Preparation

Place the socks in the shoebox.

Activity

Have children sort the socks according to matching pairs. Have them count the socks. Children can sort and resort by several categories (e.g., designs versus solids, casual versus dressy, and soft versus scratchy). Encourage the use of descriptive words as the children discuss how the socks look and feel.

A Little Something Else

Have children bring pairs of mittens or gloves from home. Encourage them to sort the gloves or mittens according to color, shape, size, and type (e.g., mittens versus gloves, thick versus thin, and solids versus designed).

Notes

• • •

STAR GAZING

Instructional Settings

Independent play

Small group (2–5 children)

Skills

Determining cause and effect

Predicting

Themes

Night and day

Light and dark

Space

Outside/Inside

Materials

- Small box with lid
- Black paint or black Contac paper
- Glow in the dark stickers (available at craft stores)
- Exacto knife

Preparation

1. Cover the outside of the box with the black paint or Contac paper.
2. Place the glow in the dark stickers on the inside of the box, including the lid.
3. Cut a small hole in the side of the box.

Activity

Open the box for a few moments for the stickers to absorb light. Close the box and let children look inside and see the stickers glowing. Next, keep the box closed for a few moments and have children predict whether the stickers will glow. Then let them look in the box. Ask children why they think the stickers do not glow. Have children discuss why the stickers glow after absorbing light and do not glow when they do not absorb light. Have children talk about the stars in the sky at night and outer space. Allow children to repeat opening and closing the lid to discover cause and effect.

A Little Something Else

Expand this activity by painting stars, moons, and space shapes on the inside of a large refrigerator box with glow-in-the-dark paint (available at most hardware stores or paint stores) and letting children "sit with the stars!" Then have children talk about how it would feel to live on the moon or be an astronaut.

Notes

SUPER SCOOPER

Instructional Settings

Independent play

Small group (2–5 children)

Skills

Recognizing/Identifying colors

Recognizing/Identifying full/empty

Developing fine-motor coordination

Counting with one-to-one correspondence

Themes

Colors

Food

Numbers

Materials

- Variety of 2" beads
- Plastic bowl with lid
- Ice cream scoop
- Cupcake tin

Preparation

Place the beads in the bowl and put the lid on.

Activity

Have a child remove the lid from the bowl. Show children how to transfer the beads from the bowl to the cupcake tin using the ice cream scoop. Encourage children to count how many beads are in each cupcake tin. Have children identify the colors of the beads. Then have children transfer the beads from the cupcake tin to the bowl using the ice cream scoop. Have children tell when the cupcake tin and bowl are full or empty. Show children how to return the beads to the bowl and cover it with the lid when finished.

A Little Something Else

Change the difficulty of this task for older children by using smaller beads and a melon baller for a scoop. Have children sort the beads by color. Cut a small piece of colored construction paper for each of the cupcake sections. Glue the construction paper in each section. Encourage children to match the colored beads with the construction paper.

Notes

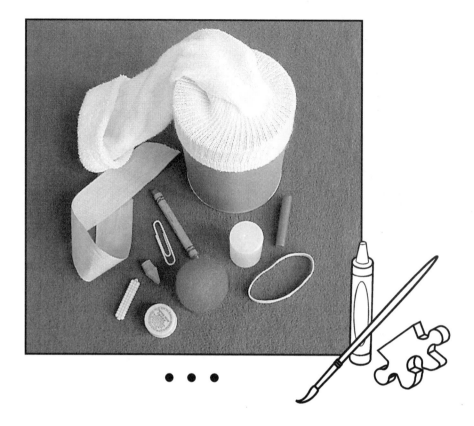

THIS FEELS LIKE...

Instructional Setting

Small group (2–5 children)

Skills

Discriminating size, shape, texture
Describing using senses
Naming objects and their functions
Predicting

Themes

Senses
Multiple themes

Materials

- Clean, dry 2 lb. coffee can
- Colored Contac paper
- Scissors
- Old knee-high sock
- Clear, wide packing tape
- Variety of objects (e.g., ball, clothespin, crayon, paintbrush, puzzle piece, marker top, clip-on earring, small dog biscuit, doll shoe, hair clip, ribbon, paper clip, large eraser, and small sock)

Preparation

1. Cover the can with the colored Contac paper.
2. Cut the foot part off the sock.
3. Pull the sock over the top of the coffee can, covering about one-third of the can.
4. Secure the sock to the can with the tape.
5. Place the objects in the can.

Activity

Instruct children to reach through the sock into the can and feel one of the objects. Have each child describe the object to the group, guess what the object is, show the object to the group, then tell what the object does. Help children tell the group about the object's function if needed.

A Little Something Else

Make additional cans using objects representing different themes you may be studying (e.g., for a unit on spring, use a packet of seeds, a small gardening glove, a silk flower, a leaf from a tree, and a plastic egg).

Notes

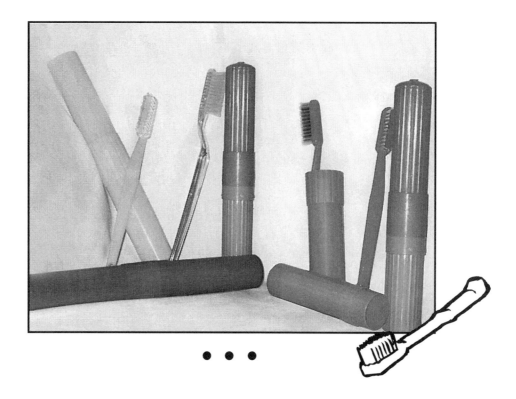

TOOTHBRUSH TANGO

Instructional Settings

Independent play
Small group (2–5 children)

Skills

Matching
Recognizing/Identifying colors
Naming objects and their functions
Naming objects by category

Themes

Health
Colors
Community helpers
Body parts

Materials

- 4–6 different colored toothbrushes (available at most Dollar Stores or free from most dental offices)
- 4–6 toothbrush travel cases in colors matching the toothbrushes (available from most Dollar stores)
- Toiletry bag

Preparation

Place the toothbrushes and the travel cases in the toiletry bag.

Activity

Show children how to match the colored toothbrushes with the corresponding colored travel cases. Encourage children to discuss how to brush teeth and what other items are needed to brush teeth. Have children talk about the type of work a dentist does. Show children how to store the toothbrushes and travel cases in the toiletry bag when finished.

A Little Something Else

Invite a dentist to talk to children about dental hygiene. Have each child bring a toothbrush from home and start a toothbrushing schedule at school.

Notes

• • •

TOUCH AND TELL

Instructional Settings

Independent play
Small group (2–5 children)
Large group (6–10 children)

Skills

Matching
Discriminating size, shape, texture
Developing fine-motor coordination
Describing using senses
Recognizing/Identifying textures
Recognizing/Identifying same/different

Themes

Senses
Outside/Inside
Clothing

Materials

- Scissors
- 6–8 scraps of material with different textures (e.g., felt, sandpaper, bubble wrap, burlap, sponge, and carpet)
- Hot glue gun
- Large (e.g., half gallon) clear plastic container with a wide opening and lid
- Fine-point permanent marker
- Velcro (available at fabric stores)

Preparation

1. Cut each scrap of material into two identical squares (approximately 2" × 2").
2. Glue one piece of each texture to the outside of the plastic container.
3. Write a descriptive word on or above each piece of texture that is on the container (e.g., *Rough, Smooth,* or *Bumpy*).
4. Glue a small piece of Velcro, soft side, on each piece of texture on the plastic container.
5. Glue a small piece of Velcro, hook side, to the backside of the remaining pieces of texture.

Activity

Encourage children to match the loose pieces of texture to the textures on the outside of the container. Have children feel the different textures and talk about them using descriptive words and the words *same* and *different*. Show children how to store the loose pieces of texture inside the container when finished.

A Little Something Else

Encourage children to find additional textures in the classroom or go for a walk outside and find items from nature with different textures.

Notes

TOUCH BOOK

Instructional Settings

Independent play
Small group (2–5 children)
Large group (6–10 children)

Skills

Describing using senses
Recognizing/Identifying textures
Recognizing/Identifying words

Themes

Senses
Clothing

Materials

- Hot glue gun
- Variety of small scraps of material with different textures (e.g., burlap, lambswool, cotton, silk, carpet, bubble wrap, sandpaper, velour, and Velcro)
- Large photo album or scrapbook with paper pages
- Fine-point permanent marker

Preparation

Glue the scraps of material, one or two to a page, in the photo album.

Activity

Let children page through the book, naming the textures as they go. Encourage the use of descriptive words (e.g., *rough, smooth, soft,* and *bumpy)* as children feel the textures and talk about them. Write children's descriptive words on the page in the photo album where the corresponding texture is glued.

A Little Something Else

Place the book in the science center or book center for children to look at independently. Place the book in the writing center, and encourage children to write words that describe the different textures.

Notes

• • •

A VERY SIMPLE COOKIE CUTTER PUZZLE

Instructional Setting

Independent play

Skills

Matching
Discriminating size, shape, texture
Recognizing/Identifying sizes
Recognizing/Identifying shapes
Ordering by size

Themes

Cookies
Food
Shapes
Holidays

Materials

- Set of 3 (small, medium, and large) identically shaped cookie cutters (available at most Dollar Stores)
- Any color poster board
- Fine-point permanent marker

Preparation

1. Set the cookie cutters on the poster board, arranging from largest to smallest.
2. Trace around the cookie cutters.
3. Laminate the poster board.

Activity

Show each child how to match the cookie cutter to the shape on the poster board. Have each child tell which cookie cutter is big, which is little, and which is medium sized. Ask what shape the cookie cutter is. Then have each child name the shape and size of each cookie cutter. Have each child order the cookie cutters from big to little and little to big without looking at the poster.

A Little Something Else

Make this more challenging by providing cookie cutters in a variety of sizes and shapes on a larger piece of poster board.

Notes

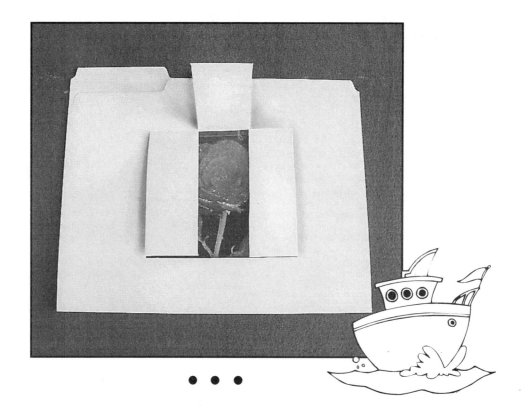

WHAT'S THAT PICTURE?

Instructional Settings

Independent play
Small group (2–5 children)

Theme

Multiple themes

Skills

Predicting
Naming objects and their functions
Recognizing part/whole

Materials

- Photographs or magazine pictures of individual objects (e.g., cat, telephone, bus, and chair)
- File folders
- Fine-point permanent marker
- Exacto knife
- Tape

Preparation

1. Lay a photograph on top of and in the center of an unopened file folder.
2. Trace around the photograph.
3. Cut around 3 of the edges of the shape to form a flap that opens.
4. Tape the photograph on the inside of the file folder to exactly correspond to the opening.
5. Cut 2 or 3 slits in the flap starting at the open end and cutting just to the closed end. (Do not cut the flap off.)
6. Laminate the file folder.
7. Cut a slit through the laminating film in the same places cut earlier.

Activity

Encourage children to predict, by naming the color, shape, or size, what the picture is as one flap is lifted at a time. Have children describe each section as it is uncovered. Have children name the object and tell what it is used for and by whom.

A Little Something Else

Change the photographs or pictures to correspond with different themes (e.g., color, farm animals, transportation, or self-awareness).

Notes

Section 2

• • •

Storytelling Activities

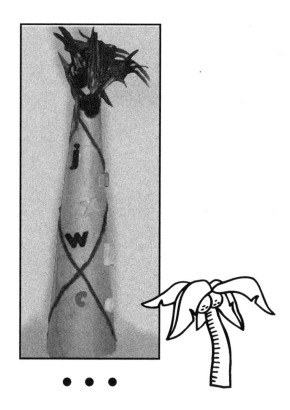

CHICKA BOOM

Instructional Settings

Small group (2–5 children)

Large group (6–10 children)

Themes

Letters

Families

Skills

Listening

Retelling a story/song/chant

Recognizing/Identifying alphabet letters

Developing sound-symbol correspondence

Materials

- Hot glue gun
- Cone-shaped piece of Styrofoam (available at craft stores)
- Three pieces of 11½" × 14" brown felt (available at craft stores)
- Brown pipe cleaners
- 8 small brown pompons (available at craft stores)
- Silk or plastic leaves
- Plastic alphabet letters (upper- and lowercase)
- Velcro strips with adhesive backing (available at craft stores)
- Small storage container
- *Chicka Chicka Boom Boom* (1989) by Bill Martin, Jr., and John Archambault, illustrated by Lois Ehlert, New York: Simon and Schuster

Preparation

1. Glue the brown felt to the Styrofoam, making the tree.
2. Glue the brown pipe cleaners around the tree for bark.
3. Glue the pompons to the top of the tree in clusters of twos or threes for coconuts.
4. Put the stem of the leaves in the top of the Styrofoam cone.
5. Adhere a small piece of Velcro, hook side, to each plastic alphabet letter.
6. Put all letters in the storage container.

Activity

Read *Chicka Chicka Boom Boom*. Place the letters on the tree as you read the story. (The Velcro will stick to the felt.) As the "tree topples down" in the story, you can easily knock the alphabet letters off the tree. Have children name the letters of the alphabet and tell the sounds each letter makes. Help children retell the story using the tree and letters. Show children how to place the letters back in the container when finished.

A Little Something Else

At snack, have children make coconut trees using brown ice-cream cones for the trees and celery leaves for the leaves. Have children use canned frosting to stick the celery leaves and alphabet cereal to the tree. Have children name each alphabet letter and the sound it makes.

Notes

• • •

FIVE GREEN AND SPECKLED FROGS

Instructional Settings

Small group (2–5 children)
Large group (6–10 children)

Skills

Listening
Developing fine-motor coordination
Counting with one-to-one correspondence
Retelling a story/song/chant
Rhyming

Themes

Ponds
Outside/Inside
Nursery rhymes

Materials

- Swag-shaped piece of Styrofoam (available in floral departments at most craft stores)
- Brown and black felt (available at craft stores)
- Scissors
- Hot glue gun
- Blue craft foam (available at craft stores)
- Five plastic frogs
- "Five Green and Speckled Frogs" chant (see pages 130–131)

Preparation

1. Cover the Styrofoam with the brown felt to create a log.
2. Cut small pieces out of the black felt for "speckles."
3. Glue the speckles on the log.
4. Cut the blue craft foam to resemble the water in a pond.

Activity

Place the frogs on the log with the pond nearby. Show children how to move the frogs into the pond one at a time as they chant "Five Green and Speckled Frogs." Encourage children to chant and manipulate the props.

A Little Something Else

Extend this activity by having children make their own frogs, pond, and log with construction paper. To add even more discovery to this activity, bring a frog into the classroom for children to observe.

Notes

Five Green and Speckled Frogs

Five green and speckled frogs

sat on a speckled log, eating the most delicious bugs. Yum, yum.

One jumped into the pool, where it was nice and cool.

Then there were four green, speckled frogs.

Glub, glub.

                              Four green and speckled frogs

              sat on a speckled log, eating the most delicious bugs. Yum, yum.

                        One jumped into the pool, where it was nice and cool.

                            Then there were three green, speckled frogs.

                                          Glub, glub.

Three green and speckled frogs

sat on a speckled log, eating the most delicious bugs. Yum, yum.

One jumped into the pool, where it was nice and cool.

Then there were two green, speckled frogs.

Glub, glub.

Two green and speckled frogs

sat on a speckled log, eating the most delicious bugs. Yum, yum.

One jumped into the pool, where it was nice and cool.

Then there was one green, speckled frog.

Glub, glub.

One green and speckled frog

sat on a speckled log, eating the most delicious bugs. Yum, yum.

He jumped into the pool, where it was nice and cool.

Then there were zero green, speckled frogs.

Glub, glub.

- - -

FLANNEL BOARD: FABRIC BOLT

Instructional Settings

Independent play

Small group (2–5 children)

Large group (6–10 children)

Theme

Multiple themes

Skills

Matching

Developing fine-motor coordination

Listening

Retelling a story/song/chant

Counting with one-to-one correspondence

Materials

- Measuring tape
- Scissors
- Black felt (available at craft stores)
- Cardboard fabric-bolt holder (available free or for a minimal cost from most fabric stores)
- Spray adhesive (available at craft stores and fabric stores)
- Various flannel-board figures

Preparation

1. Measure and cut the black felt to fit around the bolt completely.
2. Apply the spray adhesive to the bolt.
3. Gently lay the felt piece on the bolt, smooth, and allow to dry.

Activity

Provide a variety of flannel-board figures for children to manipulate match, count, compare, and contrast. Show children how to use the flannel board to tell stories. Have them listen to each other retell a story.

A Little Something Else

In the art area, provide an assortment of felt for children to make their own felt pieces or shapes to use on the flannel board. Use the felt shapes to tell stories.

Notes

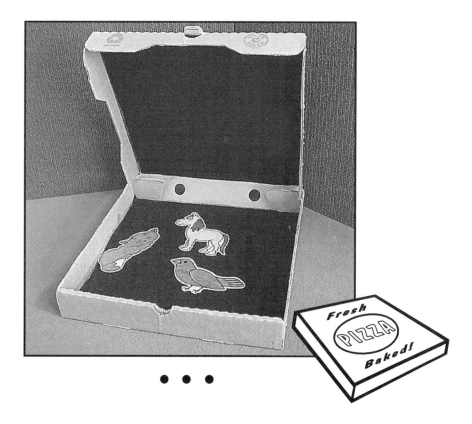

• • •

FLANNEL BOARD: PIZZA BOX

Instructional Settings

Independent play
Small group (2–5 children)
Large group (6–10 children)

Skills

Matching
Developing fine-motor coordination
Listening
Retelling a story/song/chant
Counting with one-to-one correspondence

Theme

Multiple themes

Materials

- Measuring tape
- Scissors
- Black felt (available at craft stores)
- Clean, unused pizza box (available free from most pizza restaurants)
- Spray adhesive (available at craft stores and fabric stores)
- Various flannel-board figures

Preparation

1. Measure and cut the black felt to fit the entire inside (top and bottom) of the pizza box.
2. Apply the spray adhesive to the inside of the box.
3. Gently lay the black felt inside the box, smooth, and allow to dry.

Activity

Provide a variety of flannel-board figures for children to manipulate match, count, compare, and contrast. Show children how to use the flannel board to tell stories. Have them listen to each other retell a story.

A Little Something Else

In the art area, provide an assortment of felt for children to make their own felt pieces or shapes to use on the flannel board. Use the felt shapes to tell stories.

Notes

• • •

FLANNEL BOARD: SCHOOL-SUPPLY BOX

Instructional Settings

Independent play

Small group (2–5 children)

Large group (6–10 children)

Skills

Matching

Developing fine-motor coordination

Listening

Retelling a story/song/chant

Counting with one-to-one correspondence

Theme

Multiple themes

Materials

- Measuring tape
- Scissors
- Black felt (available at craft stores)
- School supply box
- Spray adhesive (available at craft stores and fabric stores)
- Various flannel-board figures

Preparation

1. Measure and cut the black felt to fit the inside top and bottom of the box.
2. Apply the spray adhesive to the inside top and bottom of the box.
3. Gently lay the black felt on the inside top and bottom of the box, smooth, and allow to dry.

Activity

Provide a variety of flannel-board figures for children to manipulate match, count, compare, and contrast. Show children how to use the flannel board to tell stories. Have them listen to each other retell a story.

A Little Something Else

In the art area, provide an assortment of felt for children to make their own felt pieces or shapes to use on the flannel board. Use the felt shapes to tell stories.

Notes

• • •

FLANNEL BOARD:
WALLPAPER BOOK

Instructional Settings

Independent play

Small group (2–5 children)

Large group (6–10 children)

Theme

Multiple themes

Skills

Matching

Developing fine-motor coordination

Listening

Retelling a story/song/chant

Counting with one-to-one correspondence

Materials

- Wallpaper book (available free or for a minimal cost from most wallpaper stores)
- Measuring tape
- Scissors
- Black felt (available at craft stores)
- Spray adhesive (available at craft stores or fabric stores)
- Various flannel-board figures

Preparation

1. Tear the wallpaper pages out of the book. (Save these pages and place them in the art center for children to use!)
2. Measure and cut the black felt to fit the inside cover of the wallpaper book.
3. Apply the spray adhesive to the inside cover.
4. Gently lay the black felt on the inside cover, smooth, and allow to dry.

Activity

Provide a variety of flannel-board figures for children to manipulate match, count, compare, and contrast. Show children how to use the flannel board to tell stories. Have them listen to each other retell a story.

A Little Something Else

In the art area, provide an assortment of felt for children to make their own felt pieces or shapes to use on the flannel board. Use the felt shapes to tell stories.

Notes

• • •

FOLD AND PLAY

Instructional Settings

Independent play
Small group (2–5 children)
Large group (6–10 children)

Skills

Retelling a story/song/chant
Listening

Themes

My neighborhood
Multiple themes

Materials

- Cardboard accordion-style car sun visor (available at most discount stores)
- Clear Contac paper
- Various puppets and props

Preparation

1. Unfold the sun visor and lay it flat.
2. Cover one side of the sun visor with the Contac paper.

Activity

Have children stand the sun visor up on a table or the floor. Children can use this prop as a puppet theater, storefront, or restaurant front. Show them how they can make up their own role-plays or retell stories for others to listen to using the puppets.

A Little Something Else

Encourage children to make their own puppets to use with the fold-and-play prop.

Notes

THE ITSY BITSY SPIDER

Instructional Settings

Small group (2–5 children)
Large group (6–10 children)

Skills

Developing fine-motor coordination
Listening
Retelling a story/song/chant

Themes

Insects
Seasons
Weather
Nursery rhymes

Materials

- 18" piece of PVC pipe with a 3" diameter opening or thick cardboard tube
- Aluminum foil
- Clear, wide packing tape
- Hot glue gun
- Pair of wiggle eyes (available at craft stores)
- Large pink pompon (available at craft stores)
- Scissors
- Black pipe cleaners
- Yellow craft foam (available at craft stores)
- Large yellow pompon (available at craft stores)
- 1 yard of ¼" to ½" ribbon (any color)
- Velcro strips with adhesive backing (available at craft stores)
- Blue Mylar wrapping paper
- "The Itsy Bitsy Spider" song (see page 145)
- Transparent tape

Preparation

1. Cover the PVC pipe or tube with the aluminum foil to form the waterspout.
2. Cover the foil with the packing tape, folding the tape into the inside both ends of the waterspout.
3. Glue the wiggle eyes to the pink pompon to form the spider's body.
4. Cut the pipe cleaners into 4, 6" pieces.
5. Lay 2 pipe cleaners on top of each other to form an "X" and glue them together.
6. Do the same with the other two pipe cleaners.
7. Lay one pair of pipe cleaners on top of the other pair and glue them together to make the 8 legs of the spider.
8. Fold the pipe cleaners accordion style to resemble spider legs.
9. Glue the legs to the spider's body.
10. Cut a sun with rays out of the yellow craft foam.
11. Glue the yellow pompon in the middle of the sun.
12. Lay the ribbon horizontally on a table in front of you.
13. Place the waterspout horizontally on top of the ribbon, so there is an equal amount of ribbon on each side of the waterspout.
14. Secure the ribbon to the waterspout with a small piece of transparent tape. (Remember to keep the ribbon between the table and the waterspout.)

15. Take the left end of the ribbon, thread it through the chamber of the waterspout, and pull it out the other side.

16. Take the right end of the ribbon, thread it through the chamber of the waterspout, and pull it out the other side.

17. Pull both ends of the ribbon, tighten the ribbon, then tie in a knot.

18. Cut off any excess ribbon.

19. Remove the transparent tape.

20. Glue the spider to the ribbon on the outside of the waterspout, opposite the knot.

21. Glue a small strip of Velcro, hook side, to the bottom back and bottom front of the yellow craft foam sun.

22. Glue a small strip of Velcro, soft side, to the top back of the waterspout, opposite the spider.

23. Adhere the front of the sun to the back of the waterspout.

24. Cut the blue Mylar wrapping paper into 10, $\frac{1}{8}$" × 8" strips. (This is the rain.)

25. Wrap a piece of transparent tape around one end of the Mylar strips.

26. Tape the "rain" to the inside of the waterspout, at the top and near the sun.

Activity

Sing "The Itsy Bitsy Spider" and manipulate the prop as you sing the song. Encourage children to perform the actions and sing along as you manipulate the prop (hold on to the waterspout and pull on the knot to move the spider up and down the waterspout). Then help each child take a turn manipulating the spider as the song is sung.

A Little Something Else

Bring spiders into class for children to observe web building and the life of a spider.

Notes

The Itsy Bitsy Spider

The Itsy Bitsy Spider climbed up the waterspout.
[pull the ribbon to move the spider up the waterspout]

Down came the rain
[pull the "rain" out of the waterspout]

and washed the spider out.
[pull the ribbon to move the spider down the waterspout]

Out came the sun
[turn the sun over and attach it to the waterspout]

and dried up all the rain.
[push the "rain" back into the waterspout]

And the Itsy Bitsy Spider climbed up the spout again.
[pull the ribbon to move the spider up the waterspout]

· · ·

LITTLE DUDE AND HIS FUNNY FACE

Instructional Settings

Small group (2–5 children)
Large group (6–10 children)

Skills

Recognizing/identifying colors
Developing self-awareness
Describing feelings
Listening
Retelling a story/song/chant
Developing fine-motor coordination
Describing using senses

Themes

Body parts
Numbers
Friends
Colors

146

Materials

- Hot glue gun
- 1 red and 2 fuzzy green pipe cleaners
- Small plastic megaphone (available at craft stores)
- Pair of large wiggle eyes (available at craft stores)
- Velcro (available at craft stores)
- 1 medium-sized purple, 2 large orange, and 6 small yellow pompons (available at craft stores)
- "Little Dude" (see pages 148–149)

Preparation

1. Glue the fuzzy green pipe cleaners in a squiggly manner to the top of the megaphone for hair and glue the wiggle eyes on the megaphone.
2. Glue a strip of Velcro, soft side, in the middle of the face where the nose will go and one in the middle of the face where the mouth will go.
3. At the bottom of both sides of the megaphone, place a strip of Velcro, soft side, where the toes will go, and place a strip of Velcro near the eyes where the ears will go.
4. Cut the red pipe cleaner approximately 3" long. Glue a small strip of Velcro, hook side, to the purple pompon (for the nose), the 2 orange pompons (for the ears), the 6 yellow pompons (for the toes), and the red pipe cleaner (for the mouth).
5. Attach all pieces to the megaphone.

Activity

Read "Little Dude" to children. Use the "puppet" to tell the story to the children. Help children take turns retelling the story using the puppet. Have children describe how it feels to have a friend and talk about who their friends are.

A Little Something Else

Have children make their own puppets by following a few simple steps. Give each child a large paper cup. Have children draw some eyes on the paper cup. Spray the cup with spray adhesive (available at craft stores and fabric stores) and let dry for a minute. (The adhesive will be sticky to the touch.) Encourage children to choose a mouth, ears, nose, and toes from a container of pompons. The pompons will stick to the spray adhesive. (Be careful! So will everything else!) Store children's puppets in plastic bags to keep them clean and dust free.

Notes

Little Dude

By Vicky Zimmermann and Dottie Zimmermann; based on the story "It's Soo Cold!" (1998) by Steven Woodman, Stuart, FL: The Summerland Group.

Once upon a time, there was a boy named Little Dude. One beautiful spring morning Little Dude was going to meet his friend in the park. He got dressed and ate breakfast as quickly as he could because he was anxious to start his day.

As Little Dude walked in the park, he looked at the colorful flowers, the tall tress, the kites flying high in the sky, and the sparkling pond. Little Dude found a comfortable bench (beside a trash can!) to sit on and wait for his friend.

Little Dude began to smell something stinky. "What could that be?" thought Little Dude.

The smell got stronger, and stronger, and STRONGER until finally Little Dude took off his one purple nose and put it in his pocket.

As Little Dude waited, he noticed that a nearby machine was making a lot of noise. The noise got louder, and louder, and LOUDER until finally Little Dude took off his two orange ears and put them in his pocket.

While Little Dude waited, he began to get very thirsty. He decided to buy some lemonade. Little Dude took one sip of the lemonade. It was very sour. He took another sip of the lemonade and it was very, very sour. Finally, he swallowed the last of the lemonade and it was so SOUR that Little Dude took off his one red mouth and put it in his pocket.

The sun was shining very brightly that day and the sidewalk began to get hot. Little Dude's feet began to get hot! The sidewalk got hotter, and hotter, and HOTTER until Little Dude took off his six yellow toes and put them in his pocket.

Soon Little Dude's friend came and said, "Where is my friend, Little Dude?"

"I'm right here," said Little Dude.

"You can't be my friend, Little Dude. Little Dude has one purple nose, two orange ears, one red mouth, and six yellow toes," said the friend.

"Oh no! I forgot I took off my one purple nose, my two orange ears, my one red mouth, and my six yellow toes," said Little Dude. "I'll put them on now."

So Little Dude put on his one purple nose, his two orange ears, his one red mouth, and his six yellow toes and went off to play in the park with is friend.

THE LITTLE OLD LADY WHO SWALLOWED A FLY

Instructional Settings

Small group (2–5 children)
Large group (6–10 children)

Skills

Listening
Determining cause and effect
Predicting
Retelling a story/song/chant
Rhyming

Themes

Farm animals
Insects
Fairy tales

Materials

- Exacto knife
- 11" × 17" piece of heavy cardboard or foam core
- Hot glue gun
- 4" piece of heavy, clear plastic
- Items to assemble the Little Old Lady, including fabric, rickrack, buttons, yarn, and sequins
- Thin piece of wire
- Small box (approximately 6" × 4")
- Clear, wide packing tape
- *The Little Old Lady Patterns* (see Appendix B, pages 196–197)
- Heavy stock paper
- Velcro strips with adhesive backing (available at craft stores)
- "The Little Old Lady Who Swallowed a Fly" (see pages 152–153)

Preparation

1. Cut a 3½" × 2½" opening in the lower, middle section of the heavy cardboard or foam core to form the Little Old Lady's stomach. Cover the stomach hole with the plastic by gluing it to the back of the cardboard.
2. On one side of the heavy cardboard or foam core, construct the Little Old Lady using the fabric, rickrack, and buttons for her dress, yarn for her hair, and sequins for her eyes.
3. Bend the wire to make a pair of glasses and glue it on the Little Old Lady's face.
4. Cut the long side off the small box and place the open side of the box on the back of the cardboard, against the piece of plastic. Secure it in place with the packing tape.
5. Duplicate *The Little Old Lady Patterns* onto heavy stock paper.
6. Color and cut out the animal pictures; then laminate them.
7. Cut an approximately 7" strip of Velcro, hook side, and glue it to the back of the heavy cardboard or foam core.
8. Attach a strip of Velcro, soft side, to the back of each laminated animal. Secure to the back of the heavy cardboard or foam core and remove one at a time as you read the story.

Activity

Read "The Little Old Lady Who Swallowed a Fly" to the children. As they listen to the story, drop the props into the box as the Little Old Lady in the story swallows them. Encourage children to retell the story using the props. Then review the sequence and talk about why she swallowed each critter.

A Little Something Else

Have children think of other silly rhyming things the Little Old Lady could swallow.

The Little Old Lady Who Swallowed a Fly

There was an Old Lady who swallowed a fly.
[drop the fly in the box behind the clear plastic window]
I don't know why she swallowed the fly.
Oh me! Oh my!

There was an Old Lady who swallowed a spider
[drop the spider in the box behind the clear plastic window]
that wiggled and jiggled and tickled inside her.
She swallowed the spider to catch the fly.
I don't know why she swallowed the fly.
Oh me! Oh my!

There was an Old Lady who swallowed a bird.
[drop the bird in the box behind the clear plastic window]
How absurd to swallow a bird!
She swallowed the bird to catch the spider
that wiggled and jiggled and tickled inside her.
She swallowed the spider to catch the fly.
I don't know why she swallowed the fly.
Oh me! Oh my!

There was an Old Lady who swallowed a cat.
[drop the cat in the box behind the clear plastic window]
Imagine that! Swallowed a cat!
She swallowed the cat to catch the bird.
She swallowed the bird to catch the spider
that wiggled and jiggled and tickled inside her.
She swallowed the spider to catch the fly.
I don't know why she swallowed the fly.
Oh me! Oh my!

There was an Old Lady who swallowed a dog.

[drop the dog in the box behind the clear plastic window]

What a hog to swallow a dog!

She swallowed the dog to catch the cat.

She swallowed the cat to catch the bird.

She swallowed the bird to catch the spider

that wiggled and jiggled and tickled inside her.

She swallowed the spider to catch the fly.

I don't know why she swallowed the fly.

Oh me! Oh my!

There was an Old Lady who swallowed a goat.

[drop the goat in the box behind the clear plastic window]

Just opened her throat and in walked the goat.

She swallowed the goat to catch the dog.

She swallowed the dog to catch the cat.

She swallowed the cat to catch the bird.

She swallowed the bird to catch the spider

that wiggled and jiggled and tickled inside her.

She swallowed the spider to catch the fly.

I don't know why she swallowed the fly.

Oh me! Oh my!

There was an Old Lady who swallowed a cow.

[drop the cow in the box behind the clear plastic window]

I don't know how she swallowed the cow.

She swallowed the cow to catch the goat.

She swallowed the goat to catch the dog.

She swallowed the dog to catch the cat.

She swallowed the cat to catch the bird.

She swallowed the bird to catch the spider

that wiggled and jiggled and tickled inside her.

She swallowed the spider to catch the fly.

I don't know why she swallowed the fly.

Oh me! Oh my!

There was an Old Lady who swallowed a horse.

[drop the horse in the box behind the clear plastic window]

Why she's full of course!

LUNCH AT THE DELI

Instructional Settings

Small group (2–5 children)

Large group (6–10 children)

Skills

Naming objects by category

Developing fine-motor coordination

Naming objects and their functions

Describing feelings

Listening

Recognizing/Identifying words

Themes

Community helpers

Insects

Food

Materials

- *Food Patterns* (see Appendix B, pages 198–200)
- Heavy stock paper
- Scissors
- ¼" thick foam rubber (available by the yard at fabric stores)
- White, light-green, dark-green, red, orange, yellow, tan, dark-brown, and pink craft foam (available at most craft stores)
- Brown permanent marker
- Empty bread bag
- Red, white, and yellow felt (available at craft stores)
- *Deli Order* (see page 157)
- Stapler
- Brown lunch bags
- Clear, wide packing tape
- Clean, empty milk and juice boxes
- Small, empty bags from a variety of chips (e.g., corn chips, potato chips, tortilla chips, and cheese puffs)
- Wax paper or plastic sandwich bags
- Paper plates
- Napkins
- Small bell
- Pencils
- Large container

Preparation

1. Duplicate the *Food Patterns* onto heavy stock paper.
2. Cut out the *Food Patterns* to form templates.
3. Trace the bread template on the foam rubber and cut out 8–12 slices of bread. Color the edges of the foam rubber brown to resemble crust. Add brown speckles to some slices to look like whole-wheat bread.
4. Place the slices of bread in the empty bread bag.
5. Trace the pickle template on the dark-green craft foam and cut out pickle slices.
6. Trace the lettuce template on the light-green craft foam and cut out lettuce leaves.
7. Trace the tomato template on the red craft foam and cut out tomato slices; draw or cut out triangles on the pieces to resemble a tomato slice.
8. Trace the cheddar cheese template on the orange craft foam and cut out cheddar cheese slices.

9. Trace the Swiss cheese template on the white craft foam and cut out Swiss cheese slices. Cut small holes in the pieces to resemble Swiss cheese.

10. Trace the turkey template on the tan craft foam and cut out turkey slices.

11. Trace the ham template on the pink craft foam and cut out ham slices.

12. Trace the roast beef template on the dark-brown craft foam and cut out roast beef slices.

13. Trace the ketchup template on the red felt and cut out ketchup pieces.

14. Trace the mayonnaise template on the white felt and cut out mayonnaise pieces.

15. Trace the mustard template on the yellow felt and cut out mustard pieces.

16. Duplicate several of the *Deli Order* forms and staple one to each brown lunch bag.

17. With the clear, wide packing tape secure the milk and juice boxes closed.

18. Place the sandwich items, small empty bags of chips, brown lunch bags, wax paper (for wrapping sandwiches) or plastic sandwich bags, paper plates, napkins, a small bell, and pencils in the large container.

Activity

Encourage children to experiment with the materials, equipment, and jobs associated with the deli. Have one child order a sandwich while another child listens and takes the order and another child builds the sandwich. Show children how to take an order (check [✔] items) on the *Deli Order* form. Have children name each sandwich component and discuss whether they like it. Talk about the community helpers who work at restaurants and have children name other food items they might find at a deli or sandwich restaurant. Help them name sandwich restaurants in their neighborhood.

A Little Something Else

Expand this activity to include reading the book *Sam's Sandwich* (1991) by David Pelham, New York: Penguin Books. Read the story to the class. Using the foam pieces, the felt pieces, and some plastic bugs, have children make silly sandwiches!

Notes

Deli Order

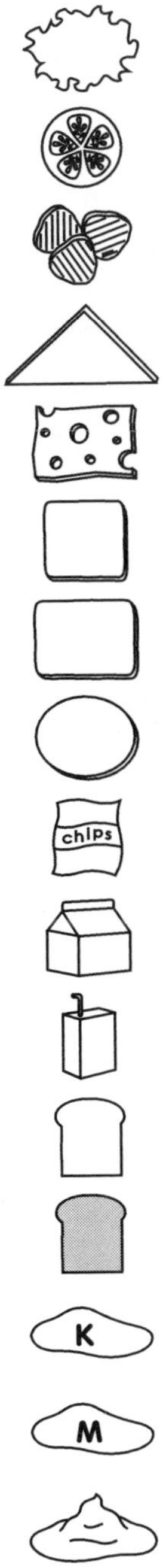

☐ Lettuce

☐ Tomato

☐ Pickles

☐ Cheddar cheese

☐ Swiss cheese

☐ Ham

☐ Roast beef

☐ Turkey

☐ Chips

☐ Milk

☐ Juice

☐ White bread

☐ Whole-wheat bread

☐ Ketchup

☐ Mustard

☐ Mayonnaise

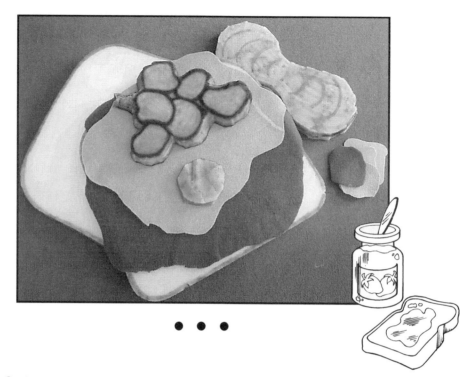

PEANUT BUTTER AND JELLY

Instructional Settings

Small group (2–5 children)
Large group (6–10 children)

Skills

Listening
Retelling a story/song/chant
Describing feelings
Developing fine-motor coordination

Theme

Food

Materials

- Scissors
- 1 yard of 1" thick foam rubber (available by the yard at fabric stores)
- Brown and purple permanent markers
- Tan and purple felt (available at craft stores)
- Bread pattern from *Food Patterns* (see Appendix B, page 198)
- Heavy stock paper
- Light-brown craft foam (available at craft stores)
- *Peanut Butter and Jelly: A Play Rhyme* (1992) illustrated by Nadine Bernard Westcott, New York: Dutton.

Preparation

1. Cut the foam rubber into 2 large (13" × 14") slices of bread. Color the outside edge of both pieces of bread brown to resemble crust.
2. Cut a 10" long peanut shape out of the foam rubber and color it brown.
3. Draw a 9" × 6" cluster of grapes on the foam; cut out the cluster and color it purple.
4. Cut the tan felt to fit the inside of the bread as peanut butter.
5. Cut the purple felt to fit the inside of the bread as grape jelly.
6. Using the foam rubber scraps, cut small peanuts and single grapes for each child.
7. Color the small peanuts brown and the small grapes purple. (Or have the children do it!)
8. Duplicate the bread pattern onto heavy stock paper.
9. Cut out the bread pattern to form a template; trace the bread pattern on the brown craft foam and cut out small slices of bread for each child. Cut out small pieces of purple and tan felt to use as peanut butter and jelly in each child's sandwich.

Activity

Read *Peanut Butter and Jelly* and tell the fingerplay at the end of the book to the class. Tell the fingerplay again, this time using the large peanut, grapes, and sandwich as props. Give each child a foam rubber peanut and grape, a felt peanut butter and jelly, and 2 pieces of foam bread. Encourage children to tell the fingerplay using the smaller food as props. Have children describe if they like peanut butter and jelly sandwiches and what kind of peanut butter and jellies they like. Graph the children's responses if desired.

A Little Something Else

Bake fresh bread and make peanut butter from scratch for a snack.

• • •

SEVEN IN THE BED

Instructional Settings

Small group (2–5 children)

Large group (6–10 children)

Skills

Developing fine-motor coordination

Listening

Counting with one-to-one correspondence

Describing feelings

Retelling a story/song/chant

Rhyming

Themes

Numbers

Night and day

Friends

Feelings

Materials

- Velcro strips with adhesive backing (available at craft stores)
- Strong, thick piece of cardboard approximately 3" × 6"
- Scissors
- Material for the blanket (e.g., flannel or fleece)
- Hot glue gun
- 14 wiggle eyes
- 6 medium-sized pompons (all the same color)
- 1 medium-sized pompon(in a different color)
- "Seven in the Bed" song (see pages 162–163)

Preparation

1. Place a strip of Velcro, soft side, horizontally across the front of the cardboard at the top.
2. Cut the material to fit the front of the cardboard piece.
3. Glue the material just under the Velcro.
4. Glue 2 wiggle eyes on each pompon.
5. Glue a small piece of Velcro, hook side, on the back of each pompon.
6. Place the pompons on the Velcro strip with the different colored pompon on the far right end.

Activity

Sing "Seven in the Bed." Perform the actions as you sing the song. Encourage children to sing along as they manipulate the story props. Have children help count the pompons as you sing. Ask children if they have ever felt lonely and, if so, what they do when they feel lonely.

A Little Something Else

Spread a blanket on the floor and have children act out the song.

Notes

Seven in the Bed

(Sing to the tune "There Were Ten in the Bed")

There were seven in the bed and the little one said, "Roll over, roll over."
So they all rolled over and one fell out. *[remove the first pompon on the left]*
There were six in the bed, and the little one said, "Why thank you, why thank you!"
[move or "roll" all the pompons to the left]

There were six in the bed and the little one said, "Roll over, roll over."
So they all rolled over and one fell out. *[remove the first pompon on the left]*
There were five in the bed and the little one said, "Why thank you, why thank you!"
[move or "roll" all the pompons to the left]

There were four in the bed and the little one said, "Roll over, roll over."
So they all rolled over and one fell out. *[remove the first pompon on the left]*
There were three in the bed and the little one said, "Why thank you, why thank you!"
[move or "roll" all the pompons to the left]

There were three in the bed and the little one said, "Roll over, roll over."
So they all rolled over and one fell out. *[remove the first pompon on the left]*
There were two in the bed and the little one said, "Why thank you, why thank you!"
[move or "roll" all the pompons to the left]

There were two in the bed and the little said, "Roll over, roll over."
So they all rolled over and one fell out. *[remove the first pompon on the left]*
There was one in the bed and the little one said, "Why thank you, why thank you!"
[move or "roll" the last pompon to the left]

There was one in the bed and the little said, "I'm lonely, I'm lonely."
So it rolled over and one jumped in. *[add one pompon]*
There were two in the bed and the little one said, "Why thank you, why thank you!"

There were two in the bed and the little said, "I'm lonely, I'm lonely."
So they all rolled over and one jumped in. *[add one pompon]*
There were three in the bed and the little one said, "Why thank you, why thank you!"

    There were three in the bed and the little one said, "I'm lonely, I'm lonely."
        So they all rolled over and one jumped in. *[add one pompon]*
  There were four in the bed and the little one said, "Why thank you, why thank you!"

There were four in the bed and the little said, "I'm lonely, I'm lonely."
So they all rolled over and one jumped in. *[add one pompon]*
There were five in the bed and the little one said, "Why thank you, why thank you!"

    There were five in the bed and the little said, "I'm lonely, I'm lonely."
        So they all rolled over and one jumped in. *[add one pompon]*
  There were six in the bed and the little one said, "Why thank you, why thank you!"

There were six in the bed and the little said, "I'm lonely, I'm lonely."
So they all rolled over and one jumped in. *[add one pompon]*
There were seven in the bed and the little one said, "Why thank you, why thank you!"

    There were seven in the bed and the little said, "I love you, I love you."
        So they all closed their eyes, and
            snored all night. Zzzz!

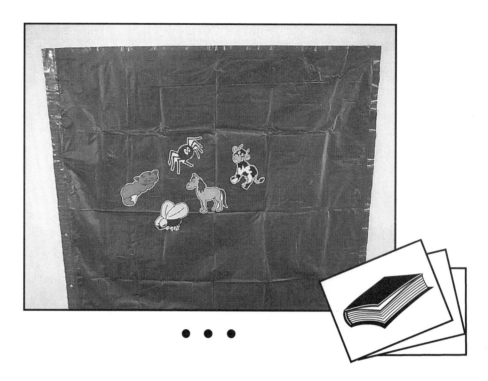

• • •

A STICKY SITUATION

Instructional Settings

Independent play
Small group (2–5 children)
Large group (6–10 children)

Skills

Describing using senses
Determining cause and effect
Recognizing/Identifying textures
Retelling a story/song/chant

Theme

Multiple themes

Materials

- Scissors
- Shower curtain liner
- Spray adhesive (available at craft stores and fabric stores)
- Clear, wide packing tape

Preparation

1. Cut the shower curtain liner to the desired size (a good size is 36" × 24").
2. Spray the shower curtain liner with the spray adhesive and let dry a few minutes.
3. Reapply the spray adhesive when the stickiness wears off.
4. Tape the shower curtain liner to the wall of your classroom with the sticky side facing out.

Activity

Paper and other lightweight objects will stick to the liner. Show children how to use the sticky sheet as a place to put artwork, stories, pictures, and story cards (see pages 168–169). Have children feel the sticky sheet and use descriptive words to tell how it feels. Have children discuss why they think the board feels the way it does.

A Little Something Else

Have children experiment with a variety of objects from the classroom and see which items will stick to the sticky sheet and which will not and speculate about why.

Notes

STORY CARD POCKET APRON

Instructional Settings

Small group (2–5 children)

Large group (6–10 children)

Skills

Listening

Developing fine-motor coordination

Retelling a story/song/chant

Theme

Multiple themes

Materials

- Scissors
- Clear plastic material (e.g., shower curtain liner)
- Apron (available at craft stores)
- Story cards (see pages 168–169)

Preparation

1. Cut the plastic piece 7" high and the width of the apron.
2. Sew the plastic piece to the apron. Use a sewing machine to sew a seam around the bottom and both sides, leaving the top open.
3. Sew 2 vertical seams in the plastic, so the apron now has 3 pockets all the same size.

Activity

Use the story card pocket apron as you read the story cards to children. Place each finished page in the pockets as you read. (You'll be covering the first 3 cards as you insert new cards.) While using the story cards and the story card pocket apron, have children retell the story, placing the cards in the apron pocket as they retell it.

A Little Something Else

Encourage children to write and illustrate their own story cards and use the story card pocket apron as they read their stories to others.

Notes

STORY CARDS

Instructional Settings

Independent play
Small group (2–5 children)
Large group (6–10 children)

Skills

Listening
Retelling a story/song/chant
Developing fine-motor coordination

Theme

Multiple themes

Materials

- Scissors
- Two copies of a children's book (e.g., Little Golden Book)
- Poster board
- Rubber cement
- Pen
- Tape recorder
- Blank audiocassette

Preparation

1. Cut out the pages of the two copies of a children's book, so you have a copy of each page.
2. Cut the poster board into cards the size of the book pages.
3. Choose which pages from the book best relate to the story.
4. Glue the pages on the cards.
5. Glue the corresponding text on the back of the cards.
6. Number the cards on the text side to keep them in order.
7. Laminate the cards.
8. Read and record the story on the audiocassette.

Activity

Read the story to children using the cards. Encourage children to retell the story using the cards. Place the story cards, audiocassette, and tape recorder in the listening center, and have children listen to the story and follow along with the story cards. (Children could place the story cards on the story card stage [see pages 170–171] if you add a strip of Velcro, hook side, to the back of each card.)

A Little Something Else

Make story cards out of class stories or individual stories that the children dictate and illustrate.

Notes

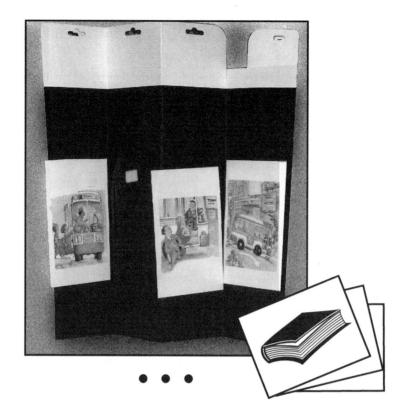

STORY CARD STAGE

Instructional Settings

Independent play

Small group (2–5 children)

Large group (6–10 children)

Skills

Developing fine-motor coordination

Listening

Retelling a story/song/chant

Theme

Multiple themes

Materials

- Cardboard accordion-style car sun visor (available at most discount stores)
- Contac paper
- Velcro strips with adhesive backing (available at craft stores)
- Story cards (see pages 168–169)

Preparation

1. Unfold the sun visor and lay it flat.
2. Cover the front side of the sun visor with the Contac paper.
3. Place a small piece of Velcro, soft side, in the middle of each section of the sun visor.
4. Place a small piece of Velcro, hook side, on the back of each story card.

Activity

As you read the story cards to children, place each finished card on a section of the story card stage (keeping the cards in order). Have children retell the story, placing the cards on the story card stage.

A Little Something Else

Use this as a display for children's artwork or encourage children to write their own stories and place them on the story card stage for display.

Notes

THREE BILLY GOATS GRUFF

Instructional Settings

Small group (2–5 children)
Large group (6–10 children)

Skills

Developing fine-motor coordination
Listening
Recognizing/Identifying sizes
Retelling a story/song/chant
Describing feelings
Predicting
Ordering by size

Theme

Fairy tales

Materials

- Straight edge
- Exacto knife
- Large piece of poster board
- Drawing pencils
- Watercolor markers or crayons
- *Three Billy Goats Gruff Patterns* (see Appendix B, pages 201–202)
- Heavy stock paper
- Scissors
- Hot glue gun
- Craft sticks
- 2, 12" rulers
- 8 Band-Aids
- "Three Billy Goats Gruff" (see page 175–176)

Preparation

1. Using the straight edge and the Exacto knife, cut a horizontal slit in the middle of the poster board leaving a 2½" margin on each side.
2. Draw and color a background scene (including a bridge) taking care that the slit is on top of the bridge, so the billy goats can "cross" the bridge.
3. Duplicate the *Three Billy Goats Gruff Patterns* onto heavy stock paper.
4. Color the figures and cut them out.
5. Laminate the figures and the background scene.
6. Cut a slit through the laminating film on the poster board in the same place that was cut earlier.
7. Glue the figures to the craft sticks to create stick puppets.
8. Glue the rulers to the backside of the poster board, at the edges, to add stability to the board.
9. On the back of the poster board, stick on 2 Band-Aids horizontally, one above the other, approximately 1" apart.
10. Do the same with the other Band-Aids, making a total of 4 groups of 2 Band-Aids.
11. Store the stick puppets on the back of the background scene by sliding the craft stick of the stick puppets into the open part of the Band-Aids.

Activity

Read "Three Billy Goats Gruff." Manipulate the stick puppets as you tell the story. Emphasize the concepts of big, medium sized, and little. Have children predict why the troll might be angry and then describe times they have felt angry. Also ask children to tell about when someone was kind to them and how that made them feel. Help children take turns retelling the story, manipulating the stick puppets, and using the size concepts as they retell it. Have them order the goat stick puppets by size.

A Little Something Else

Make similar storyboards for "Jack and the Beanstalk" and "Gingerbread Man." Follow the same directions for making the stick puppets. Cut a vertical slit in the background scene for the "Jack and the Beanstalk" story and a horizontal, curvy slit in the background scene for the "Gingerbread Man."

Notes

Three Billy Goats Gruff

Once upon a time there were three billy goat brothers. They lived in a valley and the names of the goats were Little Billy Goat Gruff, Medium-Sized Billy Goat Gruff, and Big Billy Goat Gruff. There was very little grass in the valley where the Gruff brothers lived. They were beginning to get hungry.

On the other side of the large, rushing river was a beautiful meadow full of grass, clover, and flowers. The brothers, Little Billy, Medium-Sized Billy, and Big Billy, wanted to go over to the meadow so they could eat, and eat, and eat! The only way to get over the river was to cross an old, long, narrow bridge. Under the bridge lived an angry troll who was very mean and cranky. The brothers decided to cross the bridge one at a time.

Little Billy Goat Gruff crossed the bridge first. "Trip, Trap, Trip, Trap!" went his hoofs on the bridge.

"Who is that tripping over my bridge?" roared Troll.

"Oh, it's only me, Little Billy Goat Gruff," said Little Billy Goat Gruff in his very little voice. "I'm going over to the meadow to make myself fat."

"Oh no you're not! I'm going to gobble you up right now!"

"Pleeeassse, don't eat me up. I'm little. Wait until the second Billy Goat Gruff brother comes across the bridge. He's medium sized."

"Well, all right. You may go," said Troll.

A little later, the second brother, Medium-Sized Billy Goat Gruff, crossed the bridge. "Trip, Trap, Trip, Trap!" went his hoofs on the bridge.

"Who is that tripping over my bridge?" roared Troll.

"Oh, it's only me, Medium-Sized Billy Goat Gruff," said Medium-Sized Billy Goat Gruff in his medium-sized voice. "I'm going over to the meadow to make myself fat."

"Oh no you're not! I'm going to gobble you up right now!"

"Pleeeassse, don't eat me up. I'm medium sized. Wait until the third Billy Goat Gruff brother comes across the bridge. He's big."

"Well, all right. You may go," said Troll.

A little later, the third brother, Big Billy Goat Gruff, crossed the bridge. "TRIP, TRAP, TRIP, TRAP!" went his hoofs on the bridge. Big Billy Goat Gruff was so heavy that the bridge creaked and groaned under him.

"Who is that tripping over my bridge?" roared Troll.

"Oh, it's only me, Big Billy Goat Gruff," said Big Billy Goat Gruff in his biggest voice. "I'm going over to the meadow to make myself fat."

"Oh no you're not! I'm going to gobble you up right now," said Troll.

"Pleeeassse, don't eat me up. Would you like to come with us and eat some grass, clover, and flowers instead?" asked Big Billy Goat Gruff. No one had ever been kind to Troll and this made him feel wonderful inside.

"I would love to. Thank you for asking," said Troll (who was not as angry and cranky now).

Then Troll and Big Billy Goat Gruff went to the meadow to join Little Billy Goat Gruff, and Medium-Sized Billy Goat Gruff, and they all ate, and ate, and ate. They are probably still there yet. So snip, snap, snout, this tale's told out!

Appendices

...

Dear Families,

The following are some recyclable materials often used in class. If you have any of these items at home and would like to donate some of them, I would appreciate it.

- Fabric scraps:
    - burlap
    - canvas
    - felt
    - flannel
    - old draperies
    - old carpet pieces
    - leather
    - muslin
    - fur
    - chamois
    - upholstery
    - old towels
    - old bed linens
- Photographs
- Illustrated magazines
- Wrapping paper
- Sandpaper
- Newspaper
- Cardboard tubes from:
    - toilet paper
    - paper towels
- Cardboard
- Cigar boxes
- Shoeboxes
- Frozen food boxes
- Film canisters

- Plastic bottles, bowls, and margarine tubs
- Foam packing peanuts
- Beads
- Braiding
- Buttons
- Ribbon
- Yarn
- Spools
- Rickrack
- Sequins
- Golf tees
- Food coloring
- Contac paper
- Glue
- Rocks
- Nuts
- Pinecones
- Belts
- Hats
- Gloves
- Mittens
- Shoes

- Neckties
- Purses
- Scarves
- Stockings
- Socks
- Linoleum scraps
- Ceramic tiles
- Foil
- Steel wool
- Wire
- Chains
- Paper clips
- Tacks
- Screws
- Nails
- Rubber bands
- Sponges
- Wooden clothespins

- Plastic clothespins
- Old keys
- Wood scraps:
    beads
    blocks
    boards
    dowels
    sticks
    puzzle pieces
- Craft sticks
- Keys
- Pipe cleaners
- Rope
- Twine
- Clay
- Bottle caps
- Kitchen equipment:
    utensils
    pots and pans
    plastic dishes

Sincerely,

Patterns

Bandage Pattern

Chocolate Chip Cookie Pattern

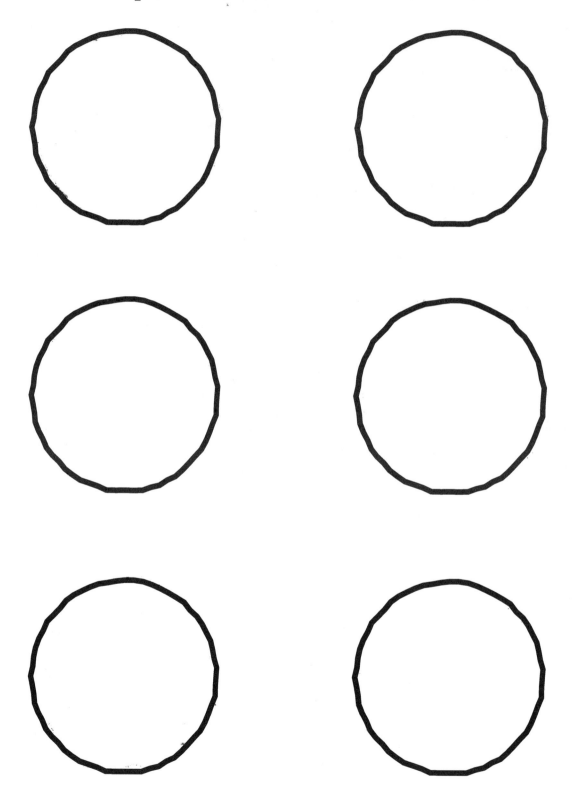

Donut Pattern

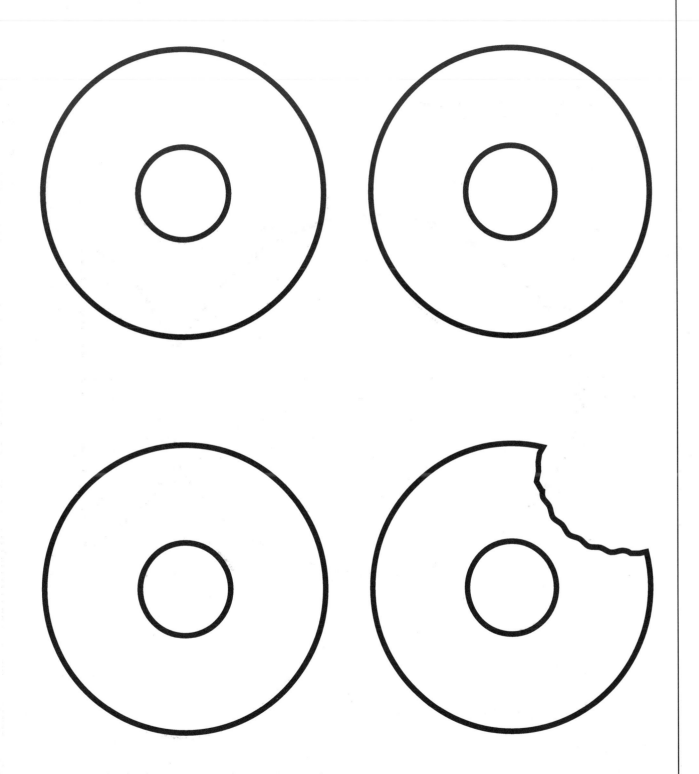

Fish Pattern

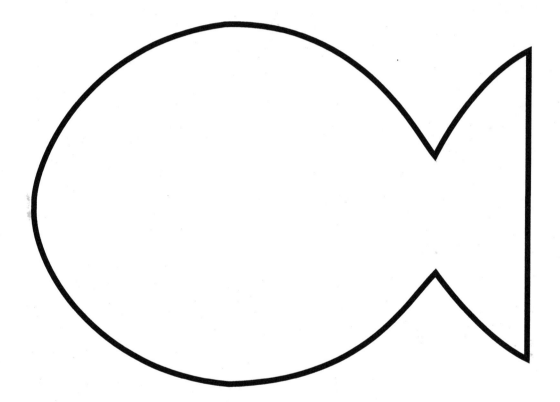

Numerals 0–5

Numerals 6–10

6 | 7

8 | 9

10

Ladybug Patterns

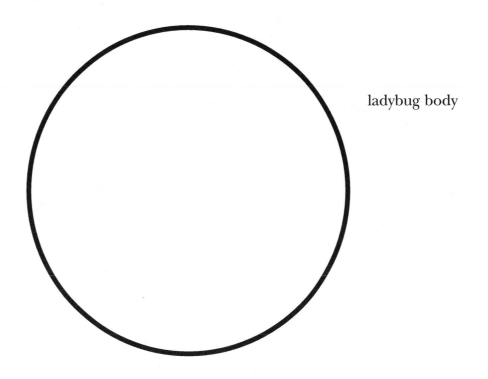

ladybug body

ladybug wings

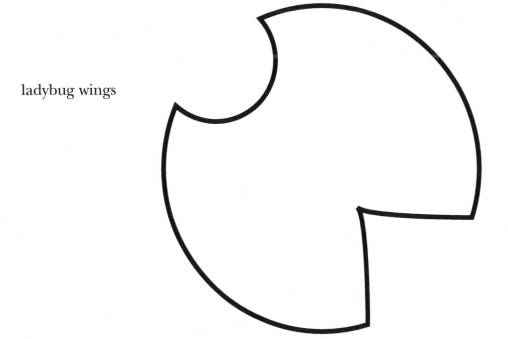

Leaf Pattern

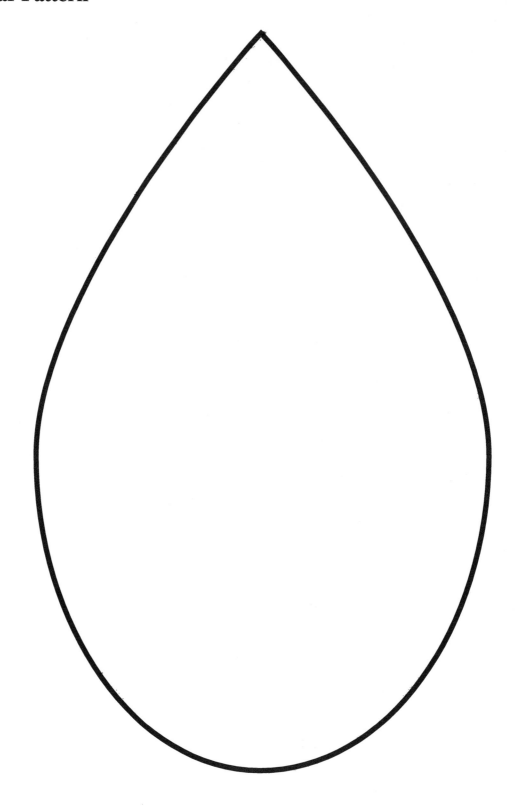

Oval Shapes

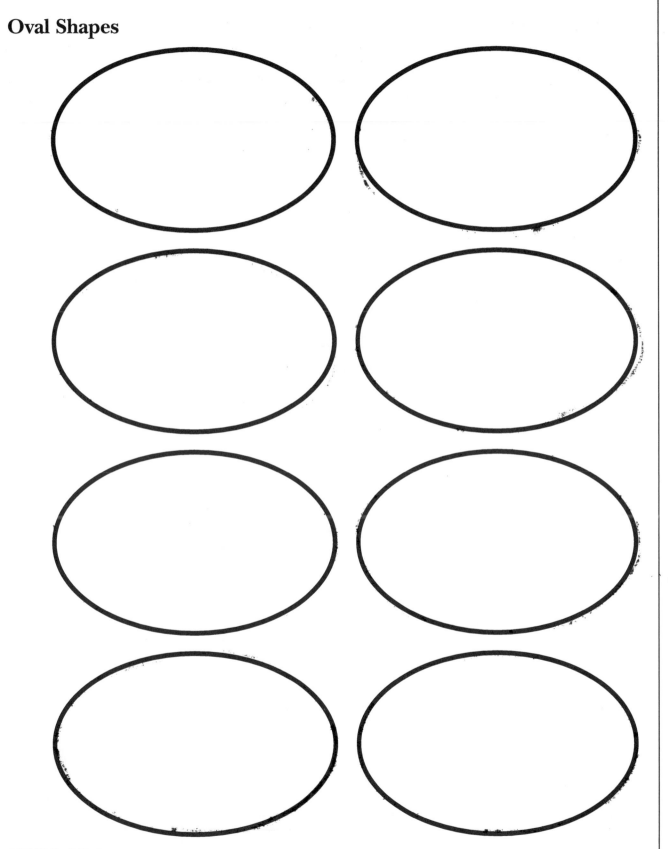

Mirror Images

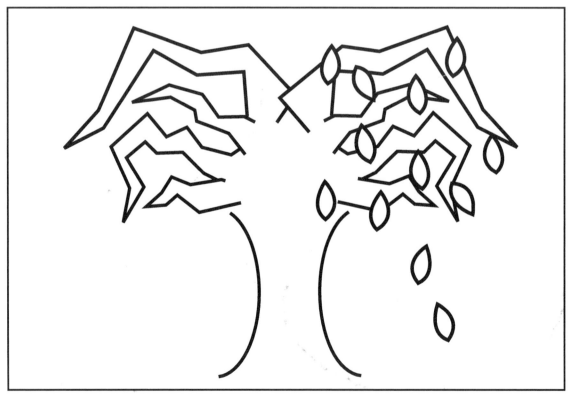

Mirror Images

Mirror Images

Gingerbread Pattern

Locations

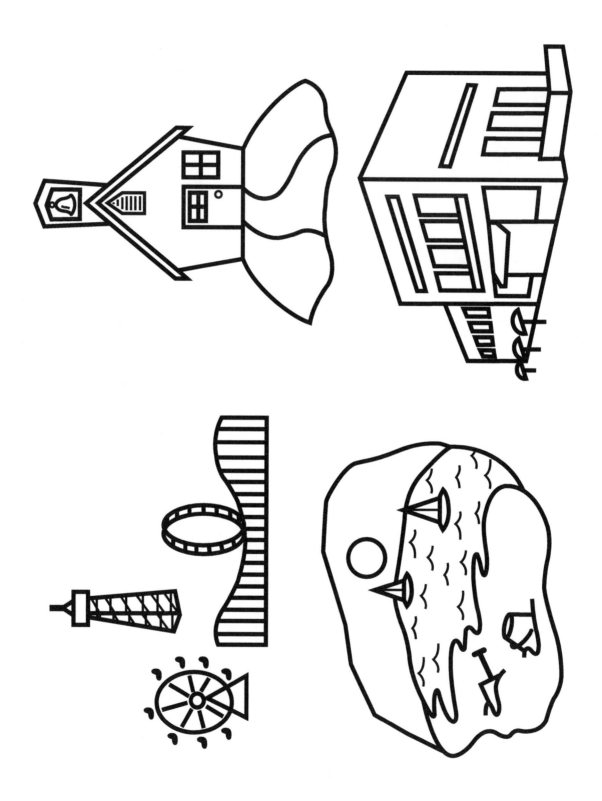

Flower Pattern

The Little Old Lady Patterns

The Little Old Lady Patterns

Food Patterns

bread

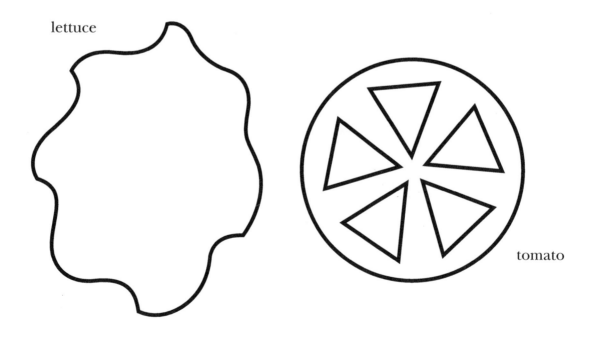

lettuce

tomato

Food Patterns

ham

Swiss cheese

turkey

roast beef

Food Patterns

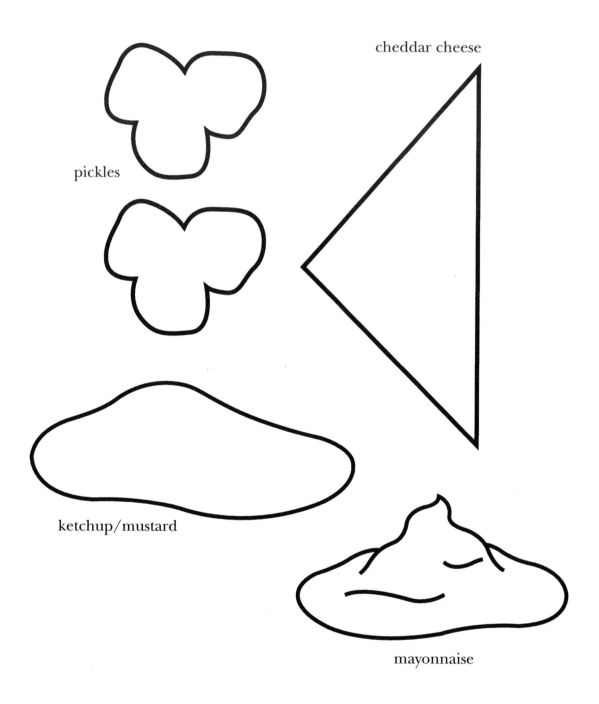

cheddar cheese

pickles

ketchup/mustard

mayonnaise

Three Billy Goats Gruff Patterns

Three Billy Goats Gruff Patterns

References

Ard, L., and Pitts, M. (1995). *Room to grow: How to create quality early childhood environments* (Rev. ed.). Austin, TX: Texas Association for the Education of Young Children.

Bernard Westcott, N. (1992). *Peanut butter and jelly: A play rhyme.* New York: Dutton.

Cryer, D., and Phillipsen, L. (1997). Quality details: A close-up look at child care program strengths and weaknesses. *Young Children, 52*(5), 51–61.

Houser, D., and Osborne, C. (no date). *Developmentally appropriate practices: Right for all kids.* Retrieved February 21, 2001, from the World Wide Web: http://www.nauti-com.net/www/cokids/dapei.html

Martin, B., Jr., and Archambault, J. (1989). *Chicka Chicka Boom Boom.* New York: Simon and Schuster.

National Association for the Education of Young Children (NAEYC). (1996a). *Benefits of an inclusive education: Making it work.* Retrieved February 21, 2001, from the World Wide Web: http://www.naeyc.org/resources/eyly/1996/07.htm

National Association for the Education of Young Children (NAEYC). (1996b). *10 signs of a great preschool.* Retrieved February 21, 2001, from the World Wide Web: http://www.naeyc.org/resources/eyly/1996/01.htm

National Association for the Education of Young Children (NAEYC). (1997). *Developmentally appropriate practice in early childhood programs serving children from birth through age 8: A position statement of the NAEYC.* Retrieved February 21, 2001, from the World Wide Web: http://www.naeyc.org/resources/position_statement/daptoc.htm

Pelham, D. (1991). *Sam's sandwich.* New York: Penguin Books.

Position statement: Developmentally appropriate practices in early childhood programs serving children birth through age eight. (no date). Retrieved February 21, 2001, from the World Wide Web: http://www.cmu.edu/cyert-center/position.html

Schultz, J. (1991). *Early childhood materials and equipment.* Wichita, KS: S.E.E.D. Publications.

Vogel, N. (1997) *Getting started: Materials and equipment for active learning preschools.* Ypsilanti, MI: High Scope Press.

Woodman, S. (1998). "It's soo cold." Stuart, FL: The Summerland Group. Retrieved March 19, 2001, from the World Wide Web: http://the-office.com/bedtime-stor/itssocold.htm